Rory MacLean's books, including best-sellers *Stalin's Nose* and *Under the Dragon*, have challenged and invigorated travel writing, and – according to the late John Fowles – are among works that 'marvellously explain why literature still lives'. He has won the Yorkshire Post Best First Work Prize and an Arts Council Writers' Award, was twice shortlisted for the Thomas Cook/Daily Telegraph Travel Book Prize and was nominated for the International IMPAC Dublin Literary award. He is a Fellow of the Royal Society of Literature and a regular contributor to BBC Radio 3 and 4. Born and educated in Canada, he lives with his family in Dorset.

'Rory MacLean is one of the most strikingly original and talented travel writers of our generation.'   Katie Hickman

Other books by Rory MacLean:

The Oatmeal Ark
Under the Dragon
Next Exit Magic Kingdom
Falling for Icarus
Magic Bus

www.rorymaclean.com

'A minor masterpiece of comic surrealism.' *The Times*

'Crazy, charming, a delight.' John le Carré

'The most extraordinary debut in travel writing since "In Patagonia". A dark, sardonic and brilliant book which grows in stature with every page.' William Dalrymple

'As an allegory it is powerful and frequently moving. As a tale it is tremendous fun. It is also a thing of beauty.' Jan Morris

'There is pathos – and adventure – in spades . . . *Stalin's Nose* is an essential companion for anyone travelling to a part of the world still recovering from the horrors of the giant confidence trick that was communism.'
Justin Marozzi, *Financial Times*

'It is a painful book of bitter old ages, or lives which have had their meanings repeatedly declared void. It is very hard and very good.' *Guardian*

'A Gogolesque tour in a Trabant: eccentric, amusing and chilling.'
The Economist

'The wittiest, most surreal travel writing of recent years.'
Frank Delaney

'The best book I've read for a long time.' John Wells

Tauris Parke Paperbacks is an imprint of I.B.Tauris. It is dedicated to publishing books in accessible paperback editions for the serious general reader within a wide range of categories, including biography, history, travel and the ancient world. The list includes select, critically acclaimed works of top quality writing by distinguished authors that continue to challenge, to inform and to inspire. These are books that possess those subtle but intrinsic elements that mark them out as something exceptional.

The Colophon of Tauris Parke Paperbacks is a representation of the ancient Egyptian ibis, sacred to the god Thoth, who was himself often depicted in the form of this most elegant of birds. Thoth was credited in antiquity as the scribe of the ancient Egyptian gods and as the inventor of writing and was associated with many aspects of wisdom and learning.

STALIN'S NOSE

Across the Face of Europe

Rory MacLean

Preface by Colin Thubron

TPP

TAURIS PARKE
PAPERBACKS

Published in 2008 by Tauris Parke Paperbacks
an imprint of I.B.Tauris & Co Ltd
6 Salem Road, London W2 4BU
175 Fifth Avenue, New York NY 10010
www.ibtauris.com

First published by HarperCollins*Publishers* in 1992
Copyright © 1992, 2008 Rory MacLean

Cover image: Painting on Berlin Wall © John Slater/CORBIS

ISBN: 978 1 84511 623 1

A full CIP record for this book is available from the British Library
A full CIP record is available from the Library of Congress

Library of Congress Catalog Card Number: available

Typeset in Bembo
Printed and bound in India by Thomson Press India Ltd

to J & R

Contents

Preface by Colin Thubron xi

If Pigs Could Fly 1

GERMANY
Let Us Eat Bananas 13

CZECHOSLOVAKIA
The Angel of Prague 29
Rooms of Memory 43
The End of Europe 58

HUNGARY
Shadows of History 73
Little Kings 81
The Moon Was Young 91

POLAND
Picnic at Auschwitz 111
May Day Parody 121
Field of Faith 138

ROMANIA
Man thinks, God laughs 153
Riding with the Best Man 169
Words Words Words 179

MOSCOVY
Communism and Constipation 189
A Pig in the Hand 208

Thanks to David Chater for starting it and
to Katrin without whom it would never have been finished.

'The one who does not remember history
is bound to live through it again'

GEORGE SANTAYANA

Preface

WITH THE PUBLICATION of *Stalin's Nose* in 1992, a new and distinctive voice sounded in the field of travel writing. By turns zany, lyrical, troubled, fantastical, Rory MacLean's first book crashed through the norms of the genre to create a surreal masterpiece. And for this burlesque tour de force the author travelled a region not of comfort but of bizarre human tragedy, as if reminding the reader that laughter arises less from happiness than from the detonations of the unexpected.

Stalin's Nose poses, too, a vital question of form: how much of it is true? Is it permissible for a travel writer to invent? And if so, how much, and in what way? Most readers take the reporter's experience on trust – for if events have been invented, they lose their power as well as their truth. Somewhere in the book, it is felt, any fictionalising must be acknowledged.

But MacLean overrides the borders between fact and fiction to create a literary species almost his own. A journey in a decrepit Trabant, in the company of a theatrically eccentric aunt, a Tamworth pig and (in Czechoslovakia) the coffin of a long-dead pilot strapped to the roof cannot be the stuff of literal reality. The reader is invited, instead, into a stark, hyper-real world. *Stalin's Nose* is not so much a travelogue as the intense distillation of a journey, and its crazy progress becomes an allegory of the tortured countries through which the travellers go. For this is the Eastern Europe of 1989-90, emerging from its Communist nightmare into a world of smoke and mirrors, confronted by its own delusions and half-truths, hypocrisies and self-blindings. Nazism and Stalinism have become interchangeable myths, bodied out in personal lives. Comedy mirrors tragedy. Moral confusion reigns.

Above all, this drama is acted out through the book's central character, the author's zestful, eccentric, belligerent aunt Zita – a faded beauty with memorably misaligned ears – who clings to the shreds of her Communism. Piece by piece her world is revealed as a moral shambles. As she and the author travel from Berlin to Prague, Brno to Budapest, they are greeted by cousins who were secret policemen, state informers, only occasionally heroes. Her brother Oto, whom Zita had adored, turns out to have been an SS officer at Auschwitz. Her husband, whose death is announced in the book's opening sentence (the Tamworth pig falls on his head) is revealed in ever blacker colours. Yet the author's affection for the mercurially human Zita shines through all her crankiness. Inhuman acts horrify him; but human beings, he seems to say, are too fragile, often too ludicrous, for the withholding of compassion.

For a while the travellers are accompanied by Zita's sister Vera, who had fought against the Nazis in the Slovak resistance, been betrayed under Communism and fled to the West. She is both Zita's opposite and mirror image, and they battle derisively against one another. In Banská Bystrica, listening to an old phonograph belonging to a cousin, they hear the voice of their long-dead brother.

'It doesn't sound anything like him.' Zita turned to Vera. 'What's he singing?' A girl's voice accompanied the song. 'And who's the warbler?'

'It's you, you're singing the SS song together,' she replied. Vera laughed the sort of laugh lovers make when confessing to infidelity. 'A Communist as a fiancé and a fascist for a brother, I don't know how you resolved that one.'

'And bloody you as a sister, that was the bugger in the wood-pile. Oto was no fascist. He was an ordinary soldier and handsome to boot.' But it wasn't true.

'Ordinary soldiers didn't volunteer for the SS.' But they did.

'Don't be ridiculous.' Zita's voice was shrill. 'Oto had no choice.' She held her throat as if to strangle herself.

The ancestry of this remarkable book is not to be found in British travel-writing. Rory MacLean is a Canadian, who started his working life as a film-maker, and he has said that it is film –

its scenic structuring and deployment of dialogue for driving a plot forward – which influenced him most potently. While still in his early twenties, a three-year stint as a film-maker in Berlin – and a voracious reading of Eastern European literature (Bulgakov, Kundera) – ignited an enduring fascination with Cold War Europe.

Early in *Stalin's Nose* he expresses his need to understand how generations of his (partly fictionalised) aunts and uncles had become, in effect, murderers. 'My forebears had killed not as individuals, as individuals they were honourable, but as groups – the Cheka, the Iron Guard, the Gestapo, the KGB – to which they had surrendered their individuality... I wanted to try to comprehend the discrepancy between the morality of a man and of men. To know how we can love someone we fear.' How do people grow blind to their human experience, clouding it with dogma, worshipping distant tyrants? 'We loved them because they freed us from the burden of self; but we feared them because with our surrender of personality they controlled us.'

But the answers to MacLean's questions, in the end, lie deep in the texture of *Stalin's Nose* itself, in its evocation of lives surrendered to phantoms, lives described with a unique mixture of comic bravado, underlying horror and a pervasive tenderness.

Colin Thubron, London

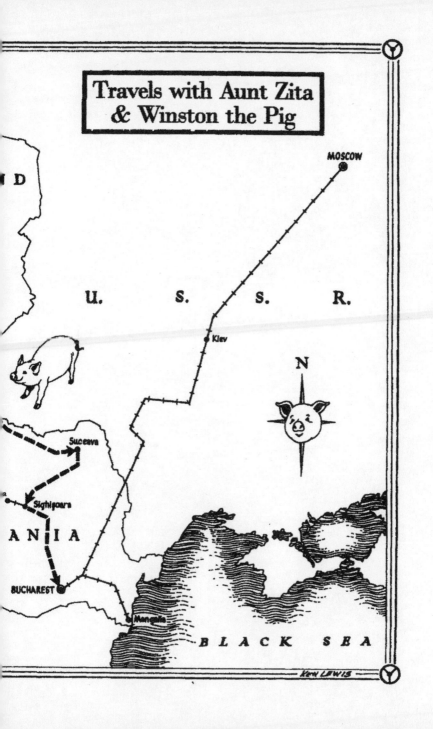

Travels with Aunt Zita
& Winston the Pig

If Pigs Could Fly

WINSTON THE PIG fell into Zita's life when he dropped onto my uncle's head and killed him dead. The news reached me in Rostock, drab, damp and winter grey, where my trip had begun. I had planned to travel from the Baltic to the Black Sea, across the continent's waist, along the line of the old Iron Curtain, but a telephone call changed everything.

'It's your uncle,' she shouted. The line was bad. I couldn't hear. Was it his legs? 'He's finally kicked buckets.' My aunt had learnt her English after the war, while the Allies remained allied, from the British military attaché in Budapest. It hadn't improved with age.

I caught the train to Berlin and changed for Potsdam. The lost corner of the West had regained its central position and Europe had reclaimed its east. The Wall, which had been open for only a few weeks, was breached in places, like a sandbank by the current, and rivers of people streamed across the false divide. They gathered in pools on no man's land, lapped against the barrier and wore it away with hammers then pocketed the detritus as mementos. The late great division of the world, between a capitalist West and a communist East, passed away as an historical aberration. Where then, if no longer down this line, was the real end of Europe?

The familiar house of white stucco and yellow shutters was hidden from the street by a thicket of hedges. 'She married a communist,' my uncle Peter had once said, 'then paints his house in papal colours.' Like the Vatican it stood as a bastion against the outside world. Battalions of change lay siege outside the garden gate but behind the evergreen wall my family defied time. Zita opened the door and Winston ran out. The murderer was grinning.

'Bloody hell, stop the beast,' she ordered over her gums. 'He's got my dentures.'

I dropped my bag and took up the chase. Zita hitched up her mourning dress. But the piglet was fast. While he skirted the flowerbeds we trampled my uncle's prized snowdrops. I dived for him, missed and tore up a patch of early crocuses. Winston squealed and grinned.

'Not the honeysuckle. Please not Peter's honeysuckle.'

But it wasn't Winston who uprooted the honeysuckle. In response to her cries Lucifer, the Dobermann, emerged from the house barking. Zita pointed at Winston but the dog, recognizing everyone except me, ignored her and tore my trousers. I fell on the honeysuckle. It was the sort of welcome I had come to expect in Potsdam.

Winston disappeared with Zita's teeth into the bracken somewhere in the lower garden. The vista had changed. Slabs of white concrete were stacked in neat piles. Barbed wire had been coiled into tumble-weed balls. The Havel lapped at the foot of the garden as it had before the Cold War. The Berlin Wall had been removed, greatly improving the view.

Zita kicked at the undergrowth. 'They pulled it down last week.' She'd noticed my surprise. 'Your uncle was furious. I told him, "It's not so bad. Now the animals can reach the water."' Then his favourite ducks swam off. It's been one of those weeks. Winston,' she shouted. 'I'll fry that ruddy pig when I find him.' Her husky voice quivered. 'Of course, it wasn't really Winston who killed him. It was the loss of the trellis.' Since 1979 Peter had grown his prize clematis up the Wall. Now a revolution had torn it down. 'What a bloody balls-up,' slurred my aunt and slumped down on the damp ground and wept.

At the funeral, which six months earlier would have drawn the high and mighty of the eastern bloc, there was only Zita, myself, Harald the gardener and Doctor Krötenschild.

'It was the angle,' explained Krötenschild with due gravity. 'Snapped his neck clean. A tragic death, of course, yet fascinating. Such a small animal.' No one knew how Winston had climbed the tree above the flower-bed where Peter had been gardening, nor from where he came, despite Harald's extensive enquiries with local farmers. He was an orphan, a runt. But like all strays my aunt took him into her heart. She fed him on milky *knödel* until he recovered from the shock. Peter, on the other hand, didn't recover. He lay in his coffin, waxen and still, the man whom I most loved.

My uncle had been a Soviet spy. He stole secrets for Stalin and changed history. My aunt was a faded Austrian aristocrat who was once considered to be the most beautiful hostess in diplomatic circles. Her defiant up-turned nose, great almond eyes and soft misaligned elephantine ears – one a full inch higher than the other – left an impression as memorable as her soirées. Princes clamoured with Party Secretaries for invitations. Then one evening an uninvited guest laid their dreams to waste.

It was at the height of his career. His toes began to tingle. Pins and needles. Two years later, while he shook hands with the head of the Polish security police, his legs collapsed beneath him. A rising star fell to earth. The doctors gave him two years to live, by which time the multiple sclerosis would have crept up his body and paralysed his heart.

Peter and Zita retreated to a rambling warren of forgotten rooms and memories on the outskirts of East Berlin. Shame closed the garden gate behind them. But instead of two years they fought the disease's advance for more than a decade, battling for every nerve and muscle. Peter walked with sticks until they splintered under his weight. He dragged himself up the stairs to his bedroom until he fell and broke both legs. He was determined to survive. Every weekend through winter's mud and summer's droughts he would wheel himself about his beloved garden, hoe in hand, secateurs jammed against a numb hip, his fingers stained silver by the cheap metal of his tools, and never utter a word of complaint. His example formed my ideal of strength and dignity.

Zita had been the toast of Prague and Moscow, the scourge of London and Washington, until her beauty faded, her hair thinned and her teeth rotted. But behind the thicket of hedges, they chose not to notice. They never went out. Harald did the weekly shop and they tended the rhododendrons. The embassy supplied the luxuries which Zita craved and she continued to cook her magnificent feasts for ambassadors who never came, for the husband who no longer ate. The animals gorged themselves on left-over truffles and smoked salmon terrine.

Zita hadn't cried at the funeral. She would cope with the loss not because of some deep inner strength but because of a lie. For Zita truth was not the facts but a matter of imagination. Facts had little bearing on her vision of reality.

She had insisted on a wake. There were so few opportunities to entertain. 'I won't do extraordinary things with the cooking,' she had said. 'You'll probably just get an omelette thrown at you. Or, better still, a cold buffet. You eat what you eat, you drink what you drink. I can't do more.' But the doctor and I were presented with the same meal which had delighted the Romanian consul in 1953. Or was it 1954? Cream of watercress soup followed by salmon en croûte and pheasant baked in cider, three types of vegetables, four salads, pommes dauphinois and Arborio rice. My aunt cooked only once or, at the most, twice a month. She would produce great banquets, whether or not guests were expected, then freeze the lot. Meals were defrosted as required, weeks or even months later. The longer the time which elapsed between visitors, the greater the caution required when sampling dishes.

The arrival of each dish was preceded by the yapping of dogs. Cats waited patiently or entwined themselves around my aunt's legs. Winston lay on the carpet in the sun. He had returned, toothless.

'But Zita,' I groaned, 'you promised only a cold buffet.'

'It's no trouble.' She gestured at a second table laden with devilled eggs, dressed crab and asparagus dipped in horseradish and wrapped in smoked salmon. It was a feast of which Zita would eat nothing. No place was set for her. She ate only in the privacy of her bedroom. Harald and the Dobermann were outside rooting through Peter's azaleas looking for teeth.

'And for the, how to say it, *la pièce de résistance*.' With great ceremony she produced a silver salver on which lay a single sizzling *bratwurst*. She smiled a gummy smile. 'For you, Winston.'

'The sausage is the most abstracted form of the pig,' Kröten-schild observed, then confided, 'Your aunt does not love all God's creatures.' Winston rose to his trotters, moved to a more inviting patch of sunlight and flopped back down on the carpet.

'I can't decide between chops or sausage meat.' Winston ignored her. Zita dislodged the threadbare basset-hound which had been snoring in her chair, slumped into the seat and lit a cigarette.

'You must eat something,' the doctor insisted. It was a familiar game. He had attended Peter for years and become their only regular guest. His digestion was remarkably resilient.

'With what?' Zita bared her gums. 'But I can bloody well drink. Ha ha.' I poured a '64 Puligny-Montrachet. 'Your uncle would hit the ceiling if he knew I was drinking his cellar dry. But, what the blazes, he's not going to miss it now.' The wine was a great improvement from the home brews of previous years. She'd stopped bottling her own vintage when all the corks blew out one hot summer's night. Zita had thought it was gunfire and hid under the bed.

'We've gone round and round in squares,' she slurred to the doctor, 'but they've gone for good. I need a new set of dentures.' The Dobermann came in and laid its head on her lap in sympathy. Harald poured himself a scotch.

'Your nephew's going to Budapest tomorrow. You should go with him.' It was common knowledge that the Hungarians were eastern Europe's best dentists.

But my plan was to travel alone. I intended writing a book on Europe in transition and explained that my stay was to be brief. My aunt wasn't particularly interested. She had noticed few changes from behind the garden gate. The years had blown away like dandelion seeds. On the walls behind her hung the portraits of her ancestors: the generations of heroic soldiers and elegant women, each with the family's distinctive misaligned ears, had been restored to their rightful place after years in the cellar. From their gilt frames watched Archduke Decimus the Handsome – with the walnut-size carbuncle – who fought Napoleon at

Austerlitz; the Countess Osyth Pomona – long thought to be infertile – who conceived the night before her husband was gassed at Passchendaele; and Oto, Zita's beloved brother, killed in the last moments of the Warsaw Uprising. Here too was her father at the opening of the Banská Bystrica silver smelter and Franz Freiherr posed in resplendent red Panduren uniform. They were all Habsburgs. At least, Zita's grandmother was a Habsburg. That is to say, her grandmother had been told she was a Habsburg – twice removed. Emperor Franz Josef never dropped by for tea but Zita's grandmother had cried at his funeral. It was she who recalled so vividly the horses with their black funereal plumes and heads bowed in respect. She had never accepted that their bridles were tethered. It was all a bit fantastic but the family history, like historical fact, read like a fiction.

Yet, for all the past glories, ours was a family divided. Dogma had diluted the bond of blood. Relatives were estranged. Zita hadn't met her sister Vera since Stalin danced at Yalta.

'I won't be in Budapest for weeks. Then I'm travelling on to Romania. In any event,' I added to dissuade, 'I'm taking the train.' For years Zita had refused to travel by train. But she wasn't listening.

'They could post me a set.'

'And guess your size?'

'Standard size. My grandfather' – Zita gestured at a portrait – 'had wooden teeth. They came in the post.' She hesitated. 'Or was it his leg?'

Krötenschild thought the trip would do her good. She shook her head. 'I can't leave the animals.'

'There are some left?' The geese, like the ducks before them, had escaped during the funeral.

'I'll have to grow another hedge,' she moaned, gesturing down the garden. East German Grenzpolizei loaded rolls of barbed wire onto a lorry. They seemed more like friendly builders than the border guards who only weeks before had shot dead an escaping Berliner. 'They wouldn't even leave a length of security fence to keep the animals in.'

She drained her glass. 'That bastard – excuse me, he was your uncle – didn't have the courtesy to live until our forty-fifth anniversary. There are only a few weeks to go and I've already done the cooking.' It would have been the second celebration of their forty-fifth anniversary. Zita had miscalculated the previous year. She had been so excited with the preparations that Peter hadn't the heart to correct her. 'He was bloody lucky to meet me, I can tell you. If he hadn't turned up I would have eloped with . . . you know.' She paused. 'What was his name?' She snapped her fingers in a vain attempt to remember.

'The beet farmer?' suggested Krötenschild.

'No. Not the beet farmer. The tall one. Oh, it doesn't matter. I should have run off with him anyway.'

'Peter used to say that were it not for him you would still be carrying pigs up mountains in Slovakia.'

'He had a problem with pigs. They made him yellow with jealousy, like old what's-his-name did.' Zita sighed, her gums hurt. She fumbled for a cigarette. 'You know, there wasn't anyone before we met. No one and nothing. There was no history. It all began on 10 May 19 . . .' She hesitated. '10 May 1947.'

'1945,' I corrected, 'and it was 9 May.' Zita had a poor memory for dates. I too had heard the stories.

'But you cannot stay here and wait to die.'

'I'm not going to bloody well die. I've got the animals.' She lit another *beuschelreißer*, a gut-tearer, and her thoughts slid away. 'Forty-five years? My God, how much older can we get?'

That night I had the sensation of falling as if I had stepped off a precipice. The soles of my feet tingled for the sure touch of earth but below me there was only emptiness, the void was bottomless and nothing would ever break my fall. Zita didn't sleep either. I heard her shuffling around her room whispering to Winston. At one point I must have dozed off for I awoke to mournful wailing but it might have been Mephisto the black howler monkey; the poor devil was an insomniac.

When I came down in the morning I imagined Peter sitting alone beneath the family portraits, looking out into the garden, his legs aching. I saw him hit them with his fist, in fury, in frustration. 'My greatest sorrow', he had once said, 'is that this leg forces me to be predictable.' But the spectre moved and

7

Harald lounged in my uncle's wheelchair. Zita appeared beside him. Her smoky slurred words sounded like footsteps on wet leaves.

'I've been up there. I've said goodbye.' 'Up there' was the animals' cemetery where her 'children', the predecessors of Lucifer and Winston, were buried.

I smelt a puff of scented powder. Zita was muffled in an unfamiliar black check suit and a skunk-skin busby. It was precisely the outfit she had worn when she last travelled – in 1979. In her gloved hand was a lead and at the end of the lead was Winston.

'I thought we could drop Harald off,' she said with a decisive air. 'It's not far out of our way.'

'I beg your pardon?'

Zita had the ability to resume conversations hours – even weeks – after they were finished. 'It's *en route* to Budapest. We'll go in the car.' Zita drove a Trabant: East Germany's contribution to civilization – a hair dryer on wheels. I doubted it would get as far as the gate.

'But it's six hundred miles to Budapest.'

'All the more reason not to drive alone.' Zita's driving was remarkably like her cooking – spectacular but dangerous. 'And Harald is a bloody liability behind the wheel.'

'What about the animals?'

'They're billeted with neighbours. You don't have to worry, things are more or less under control.' I mumbled something about my arrangements but Zita interrupted me. 'Hold it, chum. I'm your aunt. I've lost my husband and my teeth. I need looking after. Take me to the dentist then go off on your bloody train and write your ruddy book.' Her language was an endearing archaic affair, imperious Aryan command peppered with period profanity. It took some getting used to.

Harald didn't help matters. 'Never argue with an Austrian. They have an answer for everything.'

'What do you know about Austria?'

'Too much.' He continued, 'They have perfected the great deception: that Beethoven was an Austrian and Hitler a German. In fact the reverse is true.'

'Oh, shut up.' Zita preferred to accept the official version of history, that the Austrians were victims of the Third Reich. Unlike the Dobermann, her bark was worse than her bite. She had only two pegs for teeth but a protruding lower lip gave her a formidable appearance. 'My grandfather was German. My grandmother was an Austrian. I know where I stand. I landed with my bottom in butter.'

It did seem a good place for me to begin my trip, beneath the portraits, in the shadows of the devoted husbands and loving wives who – in the name of an emperor, a nation or an ideal – had committed murder. My forebears had killed not as individuals, as individuals they were honourable, but as groups – the Cheka, the Iron Guard, the Gestapo, the KGB – to which they had surrendered their individuality. Generations of aunts and uncles gave themselves to the crowd, eager to substitute irrational emotion for thought and judgment. I, a blessèd, blind baby-boomer, child of the long post-war peace, needed to understand how they had become murderers, to discover who was responsible for their unquestioning submission of self. I wanted to try to comprehend the discrepancy between the morality of a man and of men. To know how we can love someone we fear.

I pointed at the animal. 'So why is Winston on a lead?'

'So he doesn't run off, obviously. He's a gift to Harald's relatives. I can't leave him here. He'll sit quietly on the back seat with Harald. He won't be the slightest bother.'

'But he won't be allowed into hotels.'

'We'll stay with relatives. It's all arranged. Now are we going or not or what?'

We were gone.

GERMANY

GERMANY

Let Us Eat Bananas

THE GRAVEL CRUNCHED under our feet like the bones of small animals. Winston walked with confidence and grace, springing lightly on his trotters, excitement in his eye. He liked an adventure. The day was cold but clear and Zita's Trabant, with its bug eyes and beige beetle body, resembled an awkward insect overlooked by evolution. At any moment it might roll over and die. The 'go faster' stripes were particularly incongruous. A green rubber frog hung from the rear-view mirror. Winston settled beside Harald amidst the luggage on the back seat.

'Wenn der Engel reist, gibt es gutes Wetter,' he told my aunt. When the angel travels there is always good weather. The cardboard car for comrades spluttered to life. A cloud of blue two-stroke exhaust obscured our view. My offer to drive had been rejected out of hand.

'You don't know the car. You know nothing.' Miraculously the Trabant edged forward when Zita put it into gear. Its instrumentation consisted of only a speedometer. There was no fuel gauge, no horn. 'But if you play your cards right I might let you have a go on a quiet stretch of road.'

We drove out of the garden gate. The remains of the Wall followed the course of the Havel. Two elderly fishermen had hacked a hole through the concrete. They sat on the bank, rods dangling in the cold water, as they had when they were boys before Stalin had taken away their access to the river.

Slender birch saplings, in a copse beside the road, leaned together, leaned apart, like elegant dancers swaying to the music of the wind. Dressed in black and white evening dress, their branches clutched at partners, or thrust them away. We drove ten miles outside Berlin and fifty years back in time. Villages

13

were etched with tradition and grime. Cobblestone autobahns penetrated dense forests and crossed fields still tilled by hand. But the smells were not rural. Great swaths of woodland had been devastated and a forest of chimneys taken root. The road ran beside an armada of coal wagons, beneath a web of power lines and over a river stagnant with industrial effluence. Above the froth of pungent white smoke rose a furnace capped by mocking crossed hammers. But my aunt seemed only to notice the graceful church spires and small towns of ochre and burgundy.

'Out of the way, old cow,' Zita shouted and avoided a queue of traffic by mounting the kerb. Zita had never had an accident. The remarkable statistic was more a reflection of God's benevolence than of her skill. She had difficulty with the pedals. It could have been her slipped disc. She would race the engine, move off suddenly and brake hard because someone slowed down in the next lane. She accelerated when approaching a red light. 'We all die eventually,' she reasoned. It was terrifying for she didn't yet appreciate that the days had passed when the first question the police asked at the scene of an accident was 'Are you a member of the Party?' Once communists could never appear in court. In an extreme case – a fatal injury, for example – the offender would be expelled from the Party before being charged. No Party member could be convicted of a crime. Times changed and Zita had yet to learn to be a little more careful.

'It's the most extraordinary thing,' she continued as she swerved to avoid a pot-hole and missed. Winston was shaken off his perch. A hat box fell on top of him. 'My father drove me up this road when it was more or less completely new. It must have been twenty, bloody hell no, thirty years ago.'

'It might have been a little longer,' I suggested.

In fact half a century had passed since her first visit to Berlin. It had been a treat for her thirteenth birthday. Her family took their usual suite at the Aldon. The hotel concealed mysterious men and hidden doors, walk-in cupboards and dark secrets. Zita drank her first glass of champagne and flirted with an officer who taught her how to waltz. It was a double celebration. Her brother Oto was newly enlisted and on parade. From their balcony she watched him march up Unter den Linden to the Brandenburg

Gate on German Armed Forces Day. The tramp of the black columns resounded on the cobbles. Silver lacquered shoulder straps flashed in the sunlight. He looked invincible in uniform. The visit made a lasting impression.

'Excuse me but I fell in love with my brother that day. In my eye he could do no wrong.'

After the war and Oto's death she came back – with Peter – to find the hotel. It was a ruin like most of Berlin. Only the shell of the elegant building remained. A notice hung in a shattered window: 'Five o'clock tea now being served'. Tables had been set up in the cellars. The old waiters in their long formal coats and starched collars remembered the girl in pig tails and served her tea. 'No, regrettably Madame cannot have cake. There is no flour.' Or eggs. Or butter. Or sugar.

The harsh northern landscape softened. The monotonous Prussian plain rose into Thuringia's wooded hills. The Trabant puffed and wheezed up the inclines. Harald sat bolt upright, his head knocking against the low roof, happy to be going home. Winston stood on Zita's lap, his snout pressed hard against the windscreen, savouring the new smells.

When we stopped for petrol I took the opportunity to adjust the points and reset the spark plugs. Harald bought fuses and a spare fan-belt. It would be a long drive.

On the forecourt lay the wreck of a Ford Capri. Since the Wall had fallen the number of road accidents in old East Germany had risen fourfold. Initially the culprits were thought to be *Wessis* incautiously roaring down the inadequate roads. But it was the East Germans themselves who were responsible. They had forsaken their temperamental Trabants for souped-up rattletraps. But the over-powered machines were unfamiliar. The *Ossis* couldn't handle them and tended to run into things.

In the next village Harald asked Zita to stop. 'Wait here,' he said and disappeared behind a closed shop marked simply *Lebensmittel* – life means. In its window a single ice-cube tray was displayed. He returned a minute later, a case of beer under his arm. 'We will have a celebration.'

'But how . . . ?'

He tapped the side of his nose with a finger. 'Vitamin B –
bestechung.' Bribery.

'It wasn't me,' bristled Thomas, Harald's brother. 'I didn't do
it.'

Two chickens had escaped. Someone had left the gate open.
As we arrived, Thomas's wife Lotte ran through the mud in her
slippers to recapture them. Her stockings, worn in our honour,
were soiled. '*Mensch,*' she railed and started to cry. Peter's death
seemed to have upset them more than we'd anticipated.

'I never liked chickens,' Thomas added. His handshake was
cool. 'They're cruel and stupid animals but they won't let us
keep pigs any more.'

Their family had been swineherds for as long as anyone could
remember. For generations of autumns they had driven the herd
into the Buchen woods to fatten on acorns and beech-nuts. Payment at year's end was a whole pig, the intestines of another and
the tails of the rest. Pig soup had been considered a delicacy.

'The mayor can't stop us now, not after today,' chirped
Harald. It was the day of East Germany's first and last free
election, the day the people would vote their state into oblivion.
'It's fantastic, one day we're stranded in the eastern bloc, the next
– without leaving the house – we're at the heart of Europe.'
Thomas wasn't convinced.

'You're from there.' He eyed me askance. 'There' meant the
West, 'here' was the East and 'then' inferred the time before
the communists. The questions he asked were statements. My
answers he heard without listening but looked instead at my
shoes and calculated their cost.

Zita presented Winston to Thomas. 'For you.'

'I can't accept this,' he protested.

'We can begin again,' Harald told him.

During the war the brothers had tended their father's herd. In
the valley below the Buchenwald a camp had been built. Smoke
from the crematorium curled through the woods where Goethe
had written poetry. When they tired of the pigs the boys
watched the prisoners march to the underground armaments
factory. Sometimes, if they felt bold, they'd hide behind trees,

out of sight of the guards, and, as the inmates passed, draw a finger across their throats. Once a prisoner had escaped, stolen one of their piglets and hidden in the hills. The children, who knew all the best hiding places, helped the soldiers track him down.

'Peter would have liked you to have him.'

Thomas forced a laugh. His face was like an exotic fruit cleaved in two. Only a flat broad nose held the halves together and the deep furrows of his forehead turned down at right angles on either side of it. A widow's peak accentuated the division. 'Peter would have liked us to have many things.' Lotte touched her husband's hand. His widely spaced eyes squinted and he conceded, 'He was a good man. How did it happen?' Zita made a vague remark about the garden. Thomas's voice was flat. 'Peter always needed his plants.'

It was the garden which had brought our families together. In every city that they were stationed my uncle had demanded a private allotment. A gardener was always provided. But after Peter was retired no new gardener was sent. Then one day a Potsdam rubbish collector had opened the gate and asked if there were any odd jobs to do. It was Harald. Thomas, who knew and admired Peter, had sent his younger brother. Zita asked Harald what he knew about gardens. He glanced at the lush lawn and voluptuous borders and replied, 'If it were mine I'd have it paved over.' Zita hired him on the spot.

'Winston is fully house-fit so there'll be no business on the carpet,' Zita reassured Thomas. 'But, for heaven's sake, watch your dentures.' She stroked her foundling. 'He'll be much happier chasing sows around the countryside.'

'It'll be happiest on the dinner table,' said Lotte. 'We're through with breeding pigs.' Her tears had left black bruises of mascara under her eyes.

Harald laughed away the idea. Zita looked surprised. 'You're not going to eat him, are you?' The thought hadn't occurred to her.

'With bananas.' Lotte enjoyed cooking. 'All these years I have dreamed about bananas.' They had been unavailable. 'Banana pie, banana flambé, banana fruit salad: a friend in Hamburg sent me a cookbook. It was torture. The recipes called for plantains and kiwi fruit but the grocer only had turnips and apples.' The worker's paradise which had promised the world couldn't give them bananas.

'Not now, Lotte.' Thomas squeezed her shoulder; touch defused the unspoken frustration. 'It's all she eats these days.' Thomas looked at Winston. 'I don't have a pen for him.'

'We'll leave him in the car for the moment,' I suggested.

The table was laid for *abendbrot* – evening bread. Lotte brought a loaf, sausages and a bunch of bananas. Harald produced the beer and Thomas bowed his head in prayer. 'We thank Thee for Thy gifts, especially on this day . . .' Grace was interrupted by a furious banging on the floor above. 'Any news?' The muffled cry went ignored.

'Let me tell you my plan.' Harald bubbled with enterprise. 'We start small and rebuild the herd then with the profit we buy Trabants.'

'Trabants?' His brother was incredulous.

'Right. Trabants bought here and sold in the West. You get them cheaply from the factory and I'll sell them on for deutschmarks. I've got connections in West Berlin.' Harald gestured into the yard. 'Look at her; there's beauty, there's enduring design.' Zita's Trabant had a haunted look as though any moment could be its last. He stroked an imaginary contour. 'Classic lines. We used to wait fourteen years for delivery, that made us appreciate her value, now no one here wants them and that suits us fine.' He looked as pleased as a schoolboy who had recited his homework correctly.

Thomas stood, started to pour the beer then stopped and sat down again. 'I've lost my job.' He spat his words. 'After twenty-five years.' He drew his finger across his throat. 'Just like that.'

'At VEB?' It was Harald's turn for incredulity. 'But you've always worked there.'

After the war the pigherd was sent to a collective farm and Harald left to find a job in the capital. Thomas went to work at the Sachsenring Automobilwerk.

'So many people have left for the West that industry can no longer operate. A lot of companies are going to close down. The churches are empty too.' He turned to Zita. 'I was a bodywork foreman at the Trabant factory.'

'Eight and a half minutes at 170° centigrade,' his younger brother recited from memory. 'That's what you told me. Then it's slipped onto the bare chassis.' His hands embraced an imaginary waist. 'You said that it was like dressing a beautiful woman – mixed cotton frocks in summer blue and autumn green.'

'I don't remember.'

'The body's rust-proof. It's made of a combination of plastic and cotton and baked in this enormous waffle iron.' He waved his arms to illustrate its size and knocked over a lamp. Lotte caught it. 'You told me.'

'I worked hard all my life but for what?' Thomas lifted his chin, showing his throat like a beaten dog. 'I was for socialism, but the kind they taught us about in school books. The better world which Peter promised us; for peace and social progress. I served under your uncle in 1961,' Thomas reminded me. 'It was a proud moment. He was a gifted officer. None of us thought it could be done but Peter was determined. It frightened us.' The Wall my uncle built. 'I put my head in my hands and cry when I think of the waste.'

He put down the bottle. Zita couldn't quite reach it. He said, 'Now, after today, we live in hope,' but he didn't believe it. He was like a dying man who, at the end of his life, is told that his illness is cured.

'Hier ist ein toter Punkt,' said Lotte. A dead point. 'Socialism is a good idea but we'd prefer it to be tested on rats.'

'I voted today not for politics or parties but for the deutschmark,' volunteered Harald.

'I voted too.' Lotte's spirit lightened. 'While I was waiting, a man in the queue in front of me took out his penknife and scratched out a PDS sticker. You know the one that says "Courage to Dream".' PDS was the acronym of the Communist Party's new name. *Partei des Stalinismus* went the joke. 'But it still made me shiver.'

'It doesn't matter about your job,' suggested Harald. 'We can still make a go of it.'

'Maybe with someone else, not with me.'

Harald showed me our room high under the rafters, its narrow single beds smothered under thick goose-down duvets. On our way back down the stairs a door on the landing opened a crack.

'Any news?' pleaded a thin voice from the darkness.

Harald shook his head. 'None.'

'Don't lie to me. You must tell me.'

'There's no news,' he said gently and closed the door. 'Her memory's gone,' he told me, 'and the unfamiliar voices have confused her.'

Lotte was eating a banana. 'I'm sorry but I just can't stop myself.' She had been talking about her friend in Hamburg, the one with the cookbook. 'We haven't met since the war. She grew up over the road from me near Dresden. I haven't seen her for, *mensch*, forty-six years. Her family left the day before the bombing and we were supposed to follow.'

Lotte had grown up in the Erzgebirge foothills overlooking the Elbe. Her first memory was of the bombing. The valley that was Dresden burnt with her father in it. He had gone to town to arrange transportation and to take his family west, away from the advancing Russians. Even at that distance she felt the heat on her face.

'After the bombing my mother went to look for him. People had painted messages on the rubble of their houses – "*Wo ist Frau Brauert?*", "Clara Singer lies here in the ruins. Heinrich Singer now at Coswig Gardenstraβe", "Papa: we're looking for you". She never found a message.'

'I lost a cousin too.' Zita surprised me.

'My father had been selling porcelain that morning,' said Lotte. 'Two lovers playing cards. It was our only piece.' Her tears collected in little pools where her glasses rested against her cheeks. 'He had already sold it. The collector – whoever he was – hadn't enough cash. He'd asked him to come back the next day. 14 February, the day of the bombing.' She pulled a handkerchief from her pinafore apron.

Thomas found his voice. 'Why did you come here?'

'Thomas, please.'

He shook off his wife's touch. 'No. I want to know why Zita – and her nephew – have come to our house.'

'Where you are welcome, of course,' placated Lotte.

'To bring you Winston,' replied Zita, 'to give you and Harald a new start.'

'We don't need charity. You and Peter have done enough already.' A lorry passed by the window and Thomas lowered his voice. 'All these years we've lived in fear. We couldn't speak freely, not even in our own home. It's all been for nothing.' Thomas and Lotte were not heroes like my uncle. They were humble, diligent, hard-working and only wanted a peaceful life. They survived and suddenly discovered that their lives were gone.

Lotte filled the silence. 'And now Peter. Did he suffer long?'

'No. It was very quick.'

'That, at least, is a blessing. His legs was it?' she hesitated. 'A fall?'

Zita drew deeply on her cigarette. 'It was Winston. Winston fell on him.'

'What?'

'Who, not what.' She glanced toward the car.

'The pig?' asked Thomas and sniggered a twisted laugh. 'That pig killed Peter?'

'It wasn't his fault. He fell out of a tree.'

'Have you come here to torture us?' Thomas was on his feet, raging. 'You've given us the pig which broke his neck?'

'It's a gift. So we can begin again,' insisted Harald.

Lotte shook her head wildly. The pools of tears sprayed about the table. Then the frail voice from above, Lotte's mother, appeared at the door. She held a cane in her skeletal hand.

'I know you have guests but I must know if they've heard any news?'

Harald tried to comfort her. 'It's not Papa.'

Lotte's mother started to stamp the floor. 'Tell me, tell me.' Her voice shivered like a reed.

'Then the pig must die,' Thomas whispered, then shouted. 'The pig must die.' He stormed outside.

'Blow me that's cracked it,' said Zita.

When we ran outside Thomas was pounding on the car's roof, pulling at its locked doors, ranting, laughing, crying, 'Murderer! Murderer!' Inside the Trabant Winston squealed in terror. Lotte wailed. A neighbour, returning from the polling station, helped Harald to pull Thomas away. They led him back into the house. Grandmother had wrestled open a window. 'He's not coming home, is he?'

Zita turned to me, 'We'd better be off and away.'

Zita and I crossed the barren expanse of Leninplatz, the concrete heart of Dresden. Winston danced under our feet, his fear forgotten, then galloped off into the crowd.

'Hey! Winston!' barked my aunt. He turned suddenly but his hind legs continued to scamper in the original direction and he tumbled head over trotters. 'It wasn't right offering them Winston. I should have listened to the second thing in my brain.'

'Sixth sense?'

'That's it. It just felt wrong. Thomas was upset about his job. Now everything's gone to blazes.' I assumed that she meant the inconvenience of our energetic charge who was back and begging to be scratched.

'What are we going to do with him?'

'Winston? Take him with us of course. I've got his papers. No, I'd planned to stay the night with them. I didn't want to come here.'

It seemed like a place forsaken by God. The bleak, black railway station was entombed in scaffolding. Dispirited souls shuffled in the dusty evening light. They joined static queues waiting to reach a counter to be told that their request was impossible. They looked tired, their skin sallow; only alcohol brought colour to their cheeks. No one spoke above a whisper and the song of a single bird could be heard above their voices. There was no laughter but for the mocking cries of angry, drunken youths. It was Orwell's worst nightmare: a people submissive, surrendered, beaten.

Once Dresden had been Europe's baroque jewel. Canaletto came to paint its late afternoon light: skies of Prussian blue and lead white, buildings in Naples yellow and vermilion. But the combined horrors of our century – senseless destruction and soulless reconstruction – had burnt the colours away. The Royal Palace was a gutted shell, its walls sprouting weeds, the hands of its clock still arrested at the minute of the bombing. The architects had rebuilt Pragerstraβe as a desolate plain. Dresden was ashen. I asked Zita if she would like me to drive her home.

'I'm hungry and I want a bloody drink,' she proposed instead. She had made sandwiches but Winston had eaten them while we were with Thomas.

I pointed out that the kiosks were shut, it was late and we had no hotel. 'I don't think we'll find one,' I said.

'Of course we can get a beer. This is Leninplatz. He promised us. He wouldn't break his word. He was an honourable man.' I reminded her that Brutus was an honourable man too.

But we couldn't get a beer. The town was dry. No beer in Dresden. A nearby *Gaststätte* did have food but Zita lost her appetite when a great greasy knuckle of pork was dished out with pickled cabbage. Winston, stuffed with sandwiches, wouldn't even taste it. Zita complained. The waiter was not impressed. She demanded another dish. 'Surely you have something we can eat.'

'Hier, nichts,' he said and removed her plate.

Zita was furious. 'Don't you dare walk away from me, young man. I helped build this country.'

'So waren Sie es,' he said without a hint of humour. So it was you.

'I'd like to lie down with a hot water bottle,' she said wearily.

The Interhotel was joyless. The room had acrylic curtains and a view down a dingy street of dull tenements which seemed to stretch away to Warsaw. Bullet holes still scarred the crumbling façades. It was a chilling city deprived of personality – apart from the flags. They hung from every window: the West German colours, the white and green of Saxony, the yellow and black of Dynamo Dresden Football Club. 'I exist,' they dared to shout.

'*Which cousin?*' I asked.

'I've forgotten his name,' she replied. Winston slept at her feet on the foot of the bed like a heraldic hound. 'This business isn't quite what I expected. I'm sorry.'

'We'll go home tomorrow.'

She shook her head. 'I can't go back to his garden. I couldn't bear to see it without him, the weeds sprouting and the bloody bracken spreading like the blazes.' She covered her mouth as if it were a wound. 'Could we turn out the lamp?' The street-lights cast a sulphurous glow across the ceiling. Zita was quiet for a moment then addressed the gloom. 'Tomorrow I'd like to find my cousin.'

We walked alone through the Heidefriedhof, the resting place of the victims of the Allied raid. 'I like cemeteries. They're constant,' she said. Winston skipped beside my aunt like a blithe spirit. 'I've remembered his name.'

'Who?'

'My cousin Caspar.'

'Caspar?' I'd seen a photograph of Caspar. His heavy eyelids gave him the appearance of a lugubrious lizard. A protruding mouth would snap open and closed as if catching flies, although porcelain was more to his taste. During the war he had amassed an impressive collection of Meissen figurines.

'He was bloody arrogant but disciplined. I like that in a man and so do most women; you should remember that. I think it frightens us a little. He was a collector. He was collecting on the day of the bombing.'

'From refugees?' I asked.

'I couldn't tell Lotte.'

She stopped by a line of markers. 'They never found his body.' The stones were engraved: *Unbekannter, Unbekannte, Unbekannt.* Unknown man, unknown woman, unknown. 'This could be him.' She gestured at the last grave. 'But it is surprising they couldn't identify him from the ears.'

'Zita, they couldn't even tell the sex.'

She wasn't listening. 'I called the house,' she confessed, 'this morning while you were in the shower.' The water had cut off while I was washing my hair and I had heard her dialling. 'There was no one there.' She sat down on a stone and Winston settled on her lap. 'Just don't say anything but I had to be sure.'

A plastic bag of passport and vaccination certificate was extracted from her handbag. She dug deeper for another tote, this one sticky with chocolates. In a third transparent bag was a photograph of her and Peter in front of the clematis. Finally she found the road map. 'The road to Budapest goes through Brno, you know. I could show you where I grew up.'

'I'd like that,' I told her.

'And there's an old friend I'd like to look up in Prague, if you don't mind.'

I didn't mind. Peter's death and the recollection of Caspar's incineration had kindled a flame inside her. There was something new in her eyes; a hunger, perhaps. The threads of her memory spun a web across the continent. The loose ends of her life needed to be tied together and there were demons to be confronted.

For the moment my trip could take a back seat. After accompanying Zita to the dentist I planned to double-back to Poland then carry on to Romania. It wasn't a particularly logical route but my aunt needed both new teeth and familiar company. My book could wait. There were more important journeys. Austrians have big families and Zita had decided to rediscover hers.

The road snaked along the Elbe toward Czechoslovakia. On either side sandstone cliffs, weathered smooth, towered like Moorish battlements. Beneath the pinewood and birch slopes villages of brick red and Saxon yellow clung to footholds in the rock. Coal smoke hung in the air and dusted the light. The Saxons had risen from these hills to conquer and colonize. Since the middle ages the *Drängen nach Osten* had driven the Germans to the east. Again and again they had tried to possess the fertile lands of the Czechs, Poles and Rus. The last attempt had dismembered their country. But East Germany, that poor misconception, would soon be forgotten like the Despotate of Epirus and the country would be whole again.

CZECHOSLOVAKIA

The Angel of Prague

DURING THE LAST DAYS of winter a discreet black-bordered notice had appeared on Wenceslas Square. It announced the death of Strach. 'Our beloved son, father, brother and comrade,' read the solemn text, 'died aged twenty-one, after a long and serious illness. There will be no funeral rites.' The bereaved family were listed as 'Truncheons and Persecution', 'Silence and Despair'. Strach, the name of the deceased, was the Czech word for fear.

The chatter of sparrows drowned the sound of a piano echoing from an upper apartment. The birds rose in a swarm and fled into the ancient creeper which framed the windows like art nouveau metal work. On the stairs Zita told me that Karel had been 'a small power in the StB' – Státní Bezpečnost, the secret police. He knew Peter from their Moscow days.

'And, of course, there's his angel,' she said and rang the bell. The door had no number.

Angel?

'The angel of Prague.'

A laughing bear opened the door and clasped Zita. His great arms encircled her. Her slender body vanished into his embrace. He had long feminine fingers, manicured nails and hands the colour of wax. The bear, a close relative of Strach, had heard no knell.

'Do you remember,' hooted Karel as he offered Zita another vodka, 'did Peter ever tell you . . .' She refused. He poured anyway. '. . . about our attempt to recruit that Frenchman?'

'In Brno? No, Bratislava.'

The bear roared. It was safe to talk about failure with friends.

Friends? 'What a catch he would have been. We'd prepared our best Russian textbook.' A call girl. 'She was a beauty.'

'For heaven's sake get on with it.'

'She seduced him. It wasn't difficult, he had good taste. Technical Section took some classic photographs.' He rifled through a desk drawer. 'I still have them somewhere.'

'I'm not interested,' snapped Zita.

'You can't blame me for trying.'

'At our age? The world's gone to blazes and you're showing me dirty snapshots.'

'We let it ripen just enough,' he continued, 'not too much, the girl was State property after all. One day Frenchie turned up expecting his true love and found us instead. We asked him to co-operate. He refused so we showed him the photographs. And do you know the bastard liked them? He asked to keep them as a souvenir of his conquest. We threatened to send them to his wife and he offered us her address.'

He downed his glass in delight. Zita failed to hide her gums with her hand. She was relaxed in his company.

At school Karel had been a trouble-maker. He wasn't a rebel, just bored. His intelligence mocked the numbing dogma of Marxist education. He became isolated and ostracized. All he wanted was recognition. The StB noticed his talent and exploited the weakness. They offered him the chance of his life and sent him to Moscow. His individuality blossomed enforcing conformity on others. Because of men like Karel the Czech Intelligence Service became second only to the KGB in its effectiveness. Was this the man my uncle had trained?

'And how is the old man?' he asked. 'His garden wall came crashing down.'

'He's dead, Karel. I thought you'd have heard.'

Karel tugged on the lapels of his jacket as if to adjust the fit of his soul. 'I hadn't. I'm sorry.' His hand cupped Zita's wrist. 'My sources aren't what they were.'

The bottle was empty. 'Pavla?' He spoke softly to the curtain. 'Would you bring us another Stolichnaya?' The young woman who entered was less than half his age. 'You don't know Zita. Or her nephew.' She shook our hands and moved, slowly, gracefully, back toward the door. The day God made her He was having a good day. He went to bed that night pleased with His creation. 'Please stay.' The bear spoke with great tenderness.

'Of course.' She obeyed his gentle request like a command, without question, without thought. She sat beside him and, as she leaned forward to listen, her shoe slipped to expose a single chiselled heel. It was more erotic than if she had torn off all her clothes and stood naked, inviting, before us.

Karel raised his glass and proposed a toast to my uncle.

'Zitochka, I'm sorry.'

'Only Peter ever called me that.' She tugged at a thin tendril of hair and changed the subject. 'He said this new lot had booted you out.'

'He was half right. I'm being relocated but not by them. There's a post on offer in Slovakia. A different ministry, of course. It's distant enough.'

Jobs were being shuffled like playing cards and past sins swept under mats. A political commissar in the Prague police could turn up in distant Košice as a representative of the environment ministry. The old networks were still intact.

'Peter wanted to know what happened. He was like a dog with a bloody bone.'

'In November?' Karel cast a look at me. He seemed less smug and it surprised me.

'He's family,' Zita reassured him.

'I was at police headquarters – along with the KGB resident – the evening of the Národní protest.' The protest was the event which sparked the revolution and broke his Party's grip on the country. On the bitterly cold Friday afternoon some five hundred students had marched from Charles University toward Wenceslas Square, waving national flags and calling for the right of free speech. Anti-terrorist squads, in red berets, and riot police wearing white helmets fell on the protesters with tear gas and dogs. Their white wooden truncheons had metal cores. The students raised their arms and chanted, 'We have bare hands.' Hundreds were wounded in the attack.

'It looked like a complete cock-up,' suggested Zita.

'It *went* well. Very well. The police performed excellently,'

explained Karel. 'We saw the time was ripe but the Party refused
to be realistic so we acted alone; almost alone. At first it went
according to plan – I know my Czechs – but it got out of hand.
I hadn't counted on their enthusiasm. You know the saying:
more Catholic than the Pope. Now they're more democratic than
Sweden.'

By initiating the uprising the StB had hoped to control it.

'We wanted Havel to appear to be our man. The people would
reject him and we'd replace him with someone malleable. It failed
but who can tell? The seeds were planted. It may work one day.'

'The Czechs are a remarkably resilient people,' he continued,
'but they're naïve. They are like children.' Karel, a devout communist, knew in his heart that all men were not equal, that he
was more intelligent than most. The knowledge gave him a
sense of paternity. He knew better. He was the firm father who
controlled with ruthless love. 'They pretend we no longer exist
or imagine us as goblins. They believe in man's goodness but
discount his evil. They need to be protected. More vodka?' he
asked, 'or would you prefer wine?'

Even over dinner, eaten off china and drunk from crystal, the
woman hardly spoke. She wasn't withdrawn, simply not forthcoming. Her eyes would stare at us each in turn only to drop
when they were met. Behind them were veils into which I could
read nothing. She had an air of secrecy, an angelic privacy, as if
she knew what it was to fly: to spread silver wings, rise above
the roof tops and glide high in a violet sky. After supper Karel
opened the third bottle and I asked if anyone cared to join me for
a walk. His nod of approval to Pavla was almost imperceptible.

Winston had stayed in the car. Karel wasn't fond of animals.
We took him into Letenské Sady, the park where Stalin's statue
once stood. It had been the largest in the world. More Stalinist
than Stalin. Pavla was amused by Winston but reluctant to take
his lead.

'Does he bite?' she asked. I imagined that she had only seen
pigs in sausage skins. I told her that Winston's ancestors used to
be feared, that wild boar were revered by warriors and hunters.
But they damaged the crops of early settlers so, as prevention

was the best cure, the independent animals were domesticated and ever since an uneasy relationship had existed with man.

'But pigs are stupid.'

'Talk to him,' I suggested. 'He likes conversation.' Pavla knelt beside Winston and whispered endearments into his ear. The swine seemed to glow.

'Bears used to frighten me,' she said. 'When I was little I'd jump from the door to my bed without touching the floor.' In Asia it's tigers, in America monsters but in eastern Europe children fear bears under their beds. 'I'd lie between the sheets knowing they were there. Knowing that I couldn't sleep until I looked. Knowing that at the moment I did they would take me.' As they had taken her parents in 1968 when they came in tanks.

She laughed and led me to the view. Prague was cobblestones and towers, a field of copper domes gilded by the sunset. Karlův Most, the medieval Charles Bridge, spanned the Vltava. Across it, wearing bell-bottomed jeans and waving a Czech flag, her parents might have run. Soviet tanks were on the streets. Their tracks scarred the pavement. The people, unarmed, smeared them with paint. Turret guns were spiked with broomsticks. The Prague Spring, which had smelt of lilac, was crushed. Sons and daughters, mothers and fathers – the 'revisionists' – disappeared. Pavla became an orphan.

Golden Prague became the colour of dirty rust; a city of soot, scaffolding and grey Soviet uniforms. Goethe's 'prettiest gem in the stone crown of the world' wore an iron necklace of factories. The ubiquitous chimney, tip banded red and white, impaled her suburbs. Their sulphurous smoke stained her skin. Her beauty was squandered.

Pavla grew up in an orphanage under an adopted name. Until Karel claimed her. He wasn't a relation but no one raised objections for the child who didn't exist. The bear usually got his way.

'He looked after me,' she said. 'He tried to help me find my mother and father.' Without success. As we crossed the courtyard bird seed, scattered by the residents, cracked on the cobbles under our feet. 'I can't remember what they looked like.' She said no more.

'Vera's here,' Zita told me, suddenly sober. 'In Prague and everything.' She looked like she'd been slapped. The sisters hadn't met for more than forty years.

'How do you know?'

Karel answered. 'Her husband's body was found.'

'But it's unbelievable. How can she be allowed back?' asked Zita.

'She's old.' He meant she doesn't matter. 'Old and tired and times have changed. You should see her.'

'Why the blazes would I do that?' She was defensive.

'Because it's all in the past. Because she's your flesh and blood.'

'She betrayed us.'

'She wasn't the first and she certainly won't be the last.' Karel turned to me. 'Maybe we'll meet in Slovakia.'

'We're driving to Budapest,' I reminded him. They were in opposite directions.

'Vera will want to go to Slovakia and Zita will go along just to disagree with her.'

'That's completely and absolutely ridiculous,' objected my aunt.

'You two made Hitler and Stalin look like amateurs.' Pavla sat on the arm of his chair. 'Zita, see her. You've been frightened for too long.' He put his arm – his long, bloodless fingers – around the waist of the angel of Prague. She who had no past, the most beautiful woman in Czechoslovakia, leaned her head on his shoulder, as she might have rested against a cloud.

Before the revolution, when I was last in Prague, it was a city as dark as that winter's night. History had been suffocated. The Gottwald Museum smelt of cold concrete walls and heavily waxed floors. Outside, in a forgotten back alley, a man held a woman up against the wall. They were fully clothed but for the part of her skirt. As I approached he thrust himself into her. She whimpered. It was rape. I had to call the police. But then I saw the leg wrapped around him, her fingers thrust hungrily up the back of his shirt. It was love or, at least, surrender.

I wanted to believe that Pavla was a virgin, that she would

never let him have her, that she was abused not violated, pawed not penetrated. But later, after they'd retired to bed, I slipped quietly to the toilet. The muffled sounds of love-making came from behind their bedroom curtain.

'She's not a child any more. He can't imprison her.' Zita stubbed out a cigarette.

'She's living with the man who may have condemned her parents to death,' I said.

'She's free,' slurred Zita, 'like everyone.' She was thinking of Vera and asked me to rub peppermint foot lotion into her feet.

I didn't know why she stayed: out of habit, out of pity, out of fear. I thought of the friend who became so disillusioned with love that she gave herself only to strangers. When she learnt their names she would leave. No responsibilities. No demands. No expectations. Only the fear of being alone. Or was it something in Karel? The powerful understand the psychotic relationship between fear and love.

In the toilet a cockroach clung to the wall, unmoving, like the spirit of an old friend. It was there the next morning and only finally darted away when Winston tried to eat it.

One couldn't miss her. It was the ears. They were dizzily cock-eyed. Her face was laced with minute lines as fine as a spider's web. She had chipmunk cheeks and terrible teeth. When she laughed she would bite her lower lip and look away as if delight were rather naughty. But in the cellar of the National Memorial she wasn't laughing. Coffins were stacked around the shattered concrete floor where three hundred and twenty three men and her husband lay.

I knew Vera from England where she had lived in exile since the 'fifties but I hadn't seen my two aunts together. When Zita broke with the family they vowed never to meet again. They were as stubborn as they were belligerent.

Vera swept her white hair, still tinged with a memory of red, off her forehead and saw Zita. 'Your lot,' she accused.

'If you're keeping that bee in your head I'm off and away right now.'

Firemen gagged by gauze face masks lifted the caskets out of purdah. At first the dead could not be identified. They had no names, only numbers. They were Czech servicemen killed in action during the last war. Their crime was to fight for their country beside the Western Allies instead of the Russians. When the British repatriated the bodies for a heroes' funeral, the new Communist government lost them under a concrete slab; so history could relate that the Soviets were the Czechs' only ally, so school children would not be taught that the Americans liberated part of their country, so that French and Canadian paratroopers would never be honoured for giving their lives for Czechoslovakia. The truth was clean forgotten, as a dead man out of mind, forgotten but for Vera's memory and the remains of her husband, a pilot with the RAF.

She had returned to identify the body. Nightmare visions haunted her as the coffins were pried open. But the vacuum of the forgotten tomb had slowed decay. Mirek looked like a child who had slept so long and deeply that all the lines of age had vanished, the shadows gone. His skin was as smooth as marble. He appeared younger dead than the last photograph of him alive. Time played tricks in the dusty cellar and she wept.

Zita's comfort was rejected. 'You can take me back to my hotel. I want nothing else from you,' instructed Vera.

'I am your sister.'

'I have no sister. She died.'

On the journey back from Žižkov Hill Vera ignored Winston. As we drove through the Silence of Husak, the Těšnovský tunnel built along the Vltava to relieve the vast Central Committee building of traffic noise, she lifted two defiant fingers. Within the walls, the old Communists who had suffocated history now fought for breath. They waited in airless offices with nothing to do but dream. 'Keep yourselves for us,' they would tell the younger members. 'Forty years isn't a long time for an idea. Your moment will come.'

Zita bared her gums in a horrific scowl.

'It's all those Russian sweets you ate after the war,' criticized her older sister. 'I told you they'd rot your teeth.'

'It's all we could get to ear.'

'Codswallop,' pronounced Vera.

'We're going to Budapest to get new dentures.'

'I hope they arrest you. Stop the car!' Vera commanded. I stopped. Winston toppled onto the floor. She gestured at a building. 'Look familiar?'

'I've never seen the bloody place before. Drive on.'

'Don't you dare,' ordered Vera. 'I want my sister to remember.'

'Whose bloody car is this anyhow?'

'The Party's probably, unless you didn't bother with the paperwork and simply stole it.'

'I've never stolen a car in my life. Except that once.'

Sisters.

'Zita, look at it.' Zita crossed her arms and feigned fascination in a telephone pole. 'Look at it,' commanded Vera and twisted her sister's head toward the building. 'I lived there. You visited me. It's the last place we met. Remember.'

Vera had been given the flat because of her role in the Slovak resistance. It was the first room of her own with hot water, a little kitchen, even a shower – luxuries in post-war Czechoslovakia.

'Yesterday I came back for the first time in forty years. I remembered every twist in the stairs, the peculiar lift, the dark landings. I retraced my steps and rang the old doorbell but no one was home so I knocked on the next door.' She shook as she clutched Zita's head.

'A young mousy teacher used to live there but it was an old woman who opened the door. I told her I had once been a resident and we got talking about the old faces: Bibi Sander who split her drunken head on the stairs one winter, Milan Ondráček who drowned in the public pool. Then the old woman pointed at my door. "And in that flat," she said, "there was a slender girl. They were very hard on her. We had to report on her to the police. What was her name? I remember: Vera." "I am Vera," I said.'

Vera realized that the old woman was the young teacher. She saw that she too had grown old, that the forty years didn't exist, that her youth had been lost. She understood that the neighbour had betrayed her.

'When I was arrested, do you remember, Zita, I gave the key

to my secretary. She promised to look after it. All the time I was in prison I dreamt of my little flat. And my silk underwear. I had a pair of the loveliest French knickers. But when they released me she wouldn't give back my flat. "At least give me my clothes," I pleaded. "You're not wanted here," she said.' Vera slumped back in the seat. 'She later died in childbirth.' Winston had stayed on the floor. 'A very nice story. Take me to my hotel.'

I'd never heard Zita so quiet.

The proper burial of Mirek had to be arranged. An official ceremony with full military honours had been proposed. Vera had other ideas. I suggested that we discuss them over a meal but she replied, 'Why? We're not hungry. In any case, I don't have time; at my age one has to hurry.'

She wanted a private funeral but the coroner was reluctant to release the body. He maintained Mirek's remains constituted a health hazard.

'He lay under the lino for forty years. Why should he bother them now?' she snapped.

Zita offered to help. 'I have a friend,' she said.

'In any decent society all your friends would have been dismembered and their remains fed to the crows,' suggested Vera.

'I have had it up to there with your abuse and everything.'

'Then shove off. I don't need your support.'

'I'm going to help you whether you bloody well want it or not.' As a child Zita had had no playmates. Her only friends were those for whom she could do something. As she grew older she put her faith in others' beliefs for the same reason; her need to be loved.

The release was arranged within the hour. The body would be quietly discharged that evening. Zita's effort, despite her method, seemed to soften Vera.

'Having a Communist in the family', she said, 'is like having a Trabant. You don't like it but it's necessary to get on.'

A vehicle was required to pick up the coffin.

'We'll do it together,' suggested Zita.

'First thing you've ever done for me,' said Vera as she crammed her suitcase in the boot.

38

'And probably the last. Get in and shut up.'

'You must be after something.'

In the streets where history broods, close by the house where Faust sealed his pact with the devil, we found the Karlov hospital, part of Charles University. It was from the nearby medical academy that the students had marched to Národní, to meet Karel's police, to spark their velvet revolution.

Below in the hospital morgue an ancient man in a trilby with a long white beard awaited us; St Nicholas bearing unorthodox gifts. He wheeled the coffin to the car and helped me strap it to the roof. A grey tarpaulin with an elephant hide texture failed to disguise our load. 'I've seen the best come and go,' he mused. And the worst. 'In hearses, in ambulances, but never on the roof rack of a Trabant.' At the height of Stalin's purges arrested Moscovites were transported to prison in sealed bread and meat vans. Zita slipped him an envelope – Vitamin B – in which he would be surprised later to find an old Party badge.

As we drove through Soviet Tank Drivers' Square I asked for directions. 'East, of course,' said Vera. 'To Slovakia.'

Even Zita was surprised. 'But what about Mirek?'

'Because of Mirek,' retorted Vera. 'He was born there. We met there. And I'm burying him at Banská Bystrica.'

'But we can't carry a coffin across the whole bloody country,' objected Zita.

'That's typical. As usual your generosity is only skin-deep. Let me out, let us out right now. I've no time to waste arguing.'

'Stop the car,' ordered Zita. She was furious. We shuddered to a halt on the bridge. Vera clambered out over the neglected Winston and started to undo the coffin.

'I won't hold you up. I'll just untie my husband.' She gestured at the river. 'Next time you ride the Metro think of me. I built the tunnel under the Vltava.' Much of the Prague underground had been built by political prisoners. The river lapped over their labours.

'By yourself?' asked Zita, arms crossed, not moving from her seat.

'Actually a bishop helped me. Plus assorted doctors, a trade union leader and, of course, the monks.' In the early 'fifties monastic orders were dissolved. Eight thousand monks disappeared to labour camps. 'Some had been sentenced to ten years' labour.'

'Ten years?' Zita shook her head and paraphrased good soldier Svejk. 'I never imagined they'd sentence an innocent man to ten years. Sentencing an innocent man to five years, that's something I could understand, but ten; that's a bit too much.' Vera struggled with a knot. She broke a nail and started to wail. Zita snapped, 'Aren't you done yet?'

'We'll be out of your hair in a minute,' moaned Vera. I had visions of the coffin falling into the river and floating to the North Sea into which, forty years before, Mirek's Spitfire had plunged.

'Bloody hell,' cursed Zita to herself. 'Bloody bleeding hell.' She stepped out of the car, put her arm around her sister and led her to the parapet. She could easily have pushed her off, as easily as Jan Masaryk had been defenestrated in 1948. The act had cowed the Czechs. Not because the Communists murdered a liberal – political killings took place all the time – but because they assassinated the son of the founder of Czechoslovakia. The nation incarnate was strangled. They let it be known that they would do it again. 'We travel to the Soviet Union often,' the first Communist Prime Minister had told Parliament, 'as we must learn how to wring your necks.' But instead Zita said, 'We used to like each other.'

'No we didn't,' corrected Vera.

'Let's try and get on anyway.'

'What about Mirek?'

'We'll take him to Banská Bystrica.'

'But your dentures?'

She shrugged. 'I'm not too worried. I'll get them later. In addition we'll go to Brno. I want to see the old place.'

'If there's anything left.'

Winston didn't want to share his back seat. He blinked his pale eye lashes and went into a sulk.

*

Sisters. Our family had a history of quarrelling sisters. Zita and Vera were joined by blood but divided by ideology. Their mother, the gentle and loving Tamina, fell out with her sister, the Countess Osyth Pomona, when she eloped with Osyth's fiancé. Osyth never forgave Tamina. As revenge she moved to Switzerland and married a millionaire. Her aim, she claimed, was to restore the family fortune. But when the Communists nationalized Osyth's ex-fiancé's mountain and he was reduced to poverty not a centime was forthcoming.

Nor had their foremothers got on. Cantilena and Contralto, twin spinster sisters, never spoke. Yet they were so inseparable that both could claim to have borne illegitimate Decimus the Handsome who disgraced Napoleon on the fields of Austerlitz. In a close-knit family it is often difficult to tell where one member begins and another ends. Decimus himself, the carbuncled stallion, sired eight daughters. He died in his seventieth year, in his wife's arms and body, sowing the seed of Zita's great-grandmother. His girls took root across the Empire so when war and nationalism split Austro-Hungary into fragments they were separated by gulfs of misconception like a flotilla of ships scattered by storms.

Rather than earning their wealth the family tended to stumble upon it. Legend relates that an ancestor, Jan the Widower, was running from a bear when he slipped and dislodged a clod of moss. Under his feet glittered a hill of purest silver. He stood rooted to the spot, so still that the animal thought him dead and mauled his wife instead. The Kutná Hora mines made the kings of Bohemia the wealthiest sovereigns in medieval Europe.

History repeated itself when Grandfather Valtr, on honeymoon in Slovakia, took his bride in the low Tatras. In a moment of passion they tore the top soil away from another ore-rich face. Fortune smiled a third time when Václav, Zita's father, was hunting wild boar in the Brdy hills. He discovered the vein of uranium with which his country would try to build socialism. The discovery would kill him.

Silver for Polish sabres, gold for the Habsburg crown, uranium for Russian bombs; as quickly as fortunes were found, fortunes were lost. The family had a gift for backing the losing side in wars. They stood behind the Emperor when he took on Bismarck; they supported the Kaiser in 1917; they championed Masaryk's democracy between the wars. As quickly as they dug up a fortune their idealism caused them to squander it.

Morning mist veiled the low rolling fields, bare but for a single line of telephone poles which stretched to a hazy horizon. A hare harried across the road and into the hops. Copses of poplars dotted the rolling countryside south of Prague. Outside villages of red slate roofs and onion domes, winter hay was stacked in great Hovis loaves. In Příbram, a few miles west across a dry dusty plain reminiscent of Andalucia, my great-uncle's heart and back had been broken. His mines had been given to the Soviets. Over the course of a decade they sent one hundred thousand Czech political prisoners underground. Europe's greatest uranium deposits were exploited with slave labour, without payment or compensation.

'Remember,' Vera demanded of her sister.

Zita shook her head. 'That's not how it happened.' Had she forgotten or did she never know? Her memory dissipated like a mist under the sun.

Winston was fed up with being ignored. He lay his snout on Vera's lap. She looked at him askance then pushed him away. 'No children yet?' she taunted. Both had wanted children, both had been denied them.

'Catkins,' shouted Zita killing the conversation. In Peter's garden they had announced the coming of spring. We stopped to let the engine cool. Carrying the coffin was heavy work.

'They came for Papa in the night,' Vera told me, 'as they always did. They'd taken the mine and both houses. Mother was dead. There was nothing else to take. He made them wait while he shaved. I never saw him again.'

Another car had stopped under the willows. A strapping man with a full, untrimmed beard was crammed into its front seat. In his great hands he held his small blond son. He silently fed him bananas and dried figs and rubbed his whiskers over the boy's head. Zita returned from the woods with an armful of silky peach-pink blossoms. 'Moravia,' she said. 'Bloody unbelievable Moravia.'

Rooms of Memory

CZECHOSLOVAKIA WAS ONE STATE, two nations and three lands. Prague lay to the north in Bohemia, the country's ancient heart. It was here in legend that a Slav named Great-grandfather Čech settled his people. The second land, Moravia, was the Yorkshire of eastern Europe, an agricultural country of soft-spoken but determined independence. Here my forefathers had moved in the seventeenth century to escape the siege of Vienna. The family mine and foundry forged the weapons with which Jan Sobieski, the King of Poland, routed the Ottomans. But Moravia's wine, women and folk songs appealed to them and, rather than return to the Danube after the siege was lifted, they stayed in Brno for four hundred years. From the family villa my great-great-great-uncle Decimus the Handsome, after a hearty breakfast, had ridden to Austerlitz and a sort of glory. In the same garden Oto, my aunts' chivalrous brother, learnt he had been selected for duty in the Schutzstaffel. Our family's history was like a venerable ball of string, coils of emotion twined round and round, over years, over the generations.

The silhouette of medieval battlements which rose in our path was not notorious Špilberk Castle, where at least one ancestor had been imprisoned, but Bohunice, Brno new town. Ramparts of faceless apartments, devoid of individuality, barricaded the valley. Their lines were broken only by the accusing fingers of factory chimneys. Cranes like siege towers formed into ranks. The post-war years had destroyed not neighbourhoods, as in the West, but whole cities.

But Zita didn't notice. Her excitement was contagious. Winston balanced on her lap and thrust his damp pink snout out the window. The architecture did not trouble him either.

43

We drove into the old town above the monastery. In the twisting cobbled streets beneath Gothic spires and renaissance loggia, time had stood still. We parked outside a tattered villa with a tired, faded façade. As Zita opened the door the smell of gardenias filled the car. Vera elbowed past her. A crone with a face pale as wax, blue cheeks and a lie of rouge looked up from her flower bed, distant recognition in her eyes. She wheezed, 'And which one are you?'

'I'm Tamina's Vera.'

'Vera?' She embraced her with soiled hands. 'But I thought you were dead.'

'Not yet but we're optimistic,' said her younger sister.

'Zita too? Gracious God, wait until Ivo hears.'

Neither of my aunts could place the asthmatic woman. They assumed her to be of their parents' generation.

'Do you remember when we last met?' she reminded them. 'You and I were in the apple tree talking about our dreams. You wanted to see the world. I wanted babies.'

She hobbled across the courtyard to a flight of rickety stairs. Above the archway perched a double-headed Habsburg eagle. Its plumage had been plucked but its pedigree stretched back through Charlemagne to the Roman legions. The sisters were home.

The new partition walls confused Zita. 'What are all these ruddy doors?' she demanded.

'We share the house now.'

'With who?'

The woman paused to catch her breath outside the upper apartment. 'Your little cousin is going to be surprised.'

She knocked on his door but Zita pushed ahead into the tiny room. Cousin Ivo rose unsteadily to his feet. He was Moravia's great portrait photographer, a man with a profound regard for the futility of human endeavour, and his glasses were filthy. 'It's Vera and Zita,' puffed the woman.

Zita embraced Ivo and laughed. She was fourteen years old again. She leaned forward – eyes wide, lips parted, cheeks gleaming with the vitality of youth – and kissed him full on the lips. Vera kissed a partially shaved cheek.

'Hello, Ivo.'

'The two of you? Together? This is a nightmare.'

All around there were faces. Every surface was covered with portraits of moments preserved: christenings, weddings, proud soldiers in uniform – Habsburg, German, Czech, British, Soviet. The city's memories were frozen on tin plates and daguerreotypes, in silky black and white prints and gaudy colour. I walked around the room as Zita introduced me. Ivo held out his hand and spoke to the point where, a moment before, I had stood. He was blind.

'Does your nephew smell?' he whispered to Zita.

'A little,' she replied, 'but no more than Winston the pig.' Ivo's laugh was at once shy and mischievous. He smoothed his clothes with a damp palm.

'This calls for a celebration. Wine!' he demanded and a bottle was produced.

'Any diamonds yet?' asked Zita.

'Whenever I turn on the taps I hope,' answered Ivo. He turned in my direction. 'You may not know but every time Zita argued with her mother – which was not infrequently – she would flush a piece of her jewellery down the toilet.'

'The sewers of Brno run with jewels,' said the crone.

'A fortune.'

'Vera probably remembers the precise figure,' provoked Ivo. 'You always had a head for numbers. And, if you will excuse me, such lovely legs.'

'She has varicose veins now,' pointed out her sister.

'And you, Zita, you nurtured a deep sense of injustice.'

'It's not bloody surprising. After Mama died and Oto was sent away to school Vera was the one who always got everything.'

'Life simply isn't fair. The world is a sombre place with good back light,' professed Ivo. 'If only I'd known, the last time we met, that I'd never see you again.'

'Our looks haven't improved. I'd count your blessings,' said Zita. 'Where are the photographs?'

'Look around you.'

'Of the family.'

He gestured at a bureau. 'You're so forgetful. Top left. The memory drawer.'

Zita extracted a set of albums with embossed leather covers and sat cross-legged on the floor and opened them around her. She stood, in black and white, before the Brandenburg Gate. Vera in pigtails swam in Carinthia. Mirek leaned against a Spitfire. Oto posed in Nazi uniform. 'He was a bloody good-looking chap.' Zita and Peter, newly wed, embraced by the Danube, her youthful beauty preserved to mock the present.

She delved into her purse and, from among the tissues and chocolates, pulled out her Party membership card. Its photograph was recent. She passed both to me. 'So which do you prefer?' Zita aged twenty-five. Zita aged sixty-five. 'Say the wrong answer and you're out on your ear.'

Vera looked over her sister's shoulder. 'I never saw this one of Mirek.'

'He hasn't aged. This could have been taken yesterday.'

'Not with any camera I own,' said Ivo.

'He's outside, tied to the roof rack.' Ivo took it well. 'In a coffin, of course.'

'We're taking him to Banská Bystrica. Prague wasn't good enough for him,' Zita baited.

'I am dreaming,' the blind man said and shook his head.

'But I don't want him left out all night.' They explained. After waiting so long to find her husband Vera didn't want to lose him again.

'Take him to the monastery,' Ivo suggested helpfully, as if he dealt with similar problems every day. 'He can spend the night beside the ancestors. It would be rather appropriate, don't you think?'

Golden evening light warmed the terracotta roofs. Workers streamed toward trams and trains, pausing at drab shops to queue for fresh carp and bottles of Riesling labelled 'Romance'. The sullen toll of St James's bells mourned another day's passing. As dusk settled, the street lamps remained unlit. We couldn't drive through the narrow lanes to the monastery. We had to carry the coffin. Ivo and I led the way. Vera and Zita carried Mirek's feet. Bats flittered from under the eaves, above our heads, across the open-air market. Ancient Gypsies selling posies of violets crossed themselves as we passed. A woman placed a riot of wild flowers on the casket. A farmer, who had nothing else to offer, pressed a bunch of chives into Vera's hand. Others followed behind bearing improvised wreaths of pussywillows and carnations. The procession wound through the stalls toward the Capuchin monastery.

In the ventilated crypt beneath the church the Franciscans had laid their dead. The withered bodies were on the earthen floor like the poor in a destitute doss-house. Leathery skin clung to grey bones. A single eye, unhooded, suggested a wink. A curled lip mocked from the grave. Toes tensed, perfectly intact, poised as if to sprint from the afterlife. Beneath a chandelier of skulls and thigh bones lay Franz Freiherr, the ruthless Habsburg colonel who, according to family legend, had fathered Decimus. He rested on a bed of silk in a glass-topped sarcophagus. His dress uniform had crumbled into autumn leaves but his eyebrows, pronounced by sunken sockets, seemed raised in furious incomprehension. His ears were reassuringly misaligned.

At the time of Maria Theresa's succession Freiherr's name had been a byword for fear. He was an adventurer. His mother had ordered that pistols be let off near his ears to instil in him strong nerves. Hungry for adventure he joined the Russian army to fight against the Turks. He would snap Ottoman necks in his hands or, if allowed the luxury of time, pour gallons of water down his hapless captives' throats until their stomachs, grossly extended, burst. Enemy and authority alike feared him. The Czarina sentenced him to death for insubordination. Only the pleas of two ladies-of-court, to both of whom he was betrothed, granted him a reprieve at the place of execution. But they were left waiting at the respective rendezvous in their father's carriages as he took leave of their favours and Russia.

Freiherr never married. He wanted women too much to commit himself to only one. But the absence of matrimony did not restrain his procreation. His concupiscence outstripped that of his contemporary Augustus the Strong, Elector of Saxony, who sired three hundred and fifty-four acknowledged bastards.

If women were his passion, war was his love. Austria and

Prussia were battling for supremacy of the Germans. Freiherr formed the infamous Panduren-corps, a regiment of convicted criminals, whose blood-red uniforms became synonymous with terror. When they decimated Bavaria his superiors ordered him to show clemency. He reputedly replied, 'Yes, yes, a very good idea but first we will have a little garrotting.' The Austrians, who loved playing soldiers, not making war, deemed his methods unacceptable. Again he was sentenced to death but the charge was commuted to life imprisonment at Špilberk Castle where, confused and alone, he cast tin soldiers and contemplated his coffin.

Freiherr did not understand what he had done wrong. He loved and had been loved. The blood he had spilt had been in defence of the Empire and faith; at least, most of it had been. Nor did the colonel find peace in death. His head was stolen by an English collector of curiosities and sold to a circus. For one hundred years it roamed the continent accompanied by dwarfs and bearded ladies. Finally, in 1872, head and body were reunited and interned in the monastery.

We lay Mirek, his great-great-grandson-in-law, on the floor beside him. 'Sic Transit Gloria Mundi,' read the inscription. Thus departs the glory of the world.

The land around Brno was renowned for its vineyards and folk songs and Ivo had arranged an evening of music. He dressed in his finest suit; a green weave which exaggerated the tomato red of his ears. He pulled nervously at a cuff. 'Turn right at the cathedral.' The blind man gave directions. 'And left after the cemetery.' Vera and Zita, with Winston squeezed between them, brooded on the back seat.

Ivo asked, 'Have we passed the Party headquarters yet?'

'It's up ahead.'

'Carry straight on.'

We crossed an intersection. 'Smile, death is imminent,' said Zita.

Vera added, 'That was a red light.' I hadn't noticed.

'I didn't see it either,' said Ivo.

'You never paid much attention to the law,' accused Zita.

'Not true. I never did anything illegal,' he corrected her, 'but I was always sincere.'

After the demise of the new Republic in 1948 it became a liability to lack a cautious nature. Ivo had always spoken his mind and consequently was arrested for it. 'We hope you know why we are holding you,' they had told him, but no charges were laid. Three interrogators questioned him for seven hours. Their chief, an unpleasant boar with halitosis, stood over Ivo and shouted, 'We know everything.' But they knew nothing. There was nothing.

'In prison,' said Vera, 'the only way to stop the beatings was to sing the national anthem. The guards were Czechs and would stand to attention. But the warden got wise and brought in Soviets.' Zita said she remembered the tune and started to hum Aleksandrov.

Sometimes it is hard to appreciate that millions, tens of millions, one hundred million, were imprisoned, tortured or executed because they spoke their minds.

'How did it happen?' Vera asked. She meant his eyes.

Ivo shook his head. 'No. They didn't beat me. It was congenital. I would have gone blind under any system of government.'

We drove up a flight of terraces and into Nearly Nothing. Skoronice earned its name after the Thirty Years' War. The Swedish invaders had attacked the original village and left 'nearly nothing'. Ivo paused to focus his mind's eye and guide us through the dark lanes to an eclectic single-storey building.

With the headlights off the night closed around us. Ivo stepped into the street and bellowed. The unseen faces of his friends surrounded us, ushered us through the lightless alley to the heart of the house. A portal opened and we entered a bare, white, bright room. There were doors on every wall, nine in all, each closed. Extensions radiated from the original cottage like the points of a starfish. They had been tacked on according to need as time and money allowed. Zita whispered in my ear, 'Which do you think is the toilet?' In front of the doors a table groaned with food, behind the table stood our hosts.

Heda was forty-five, mother of six and pregnant with her

seventh. Luboš had won her with his alto. In Moravia the higher
a man sang the more he was admired. All the village's eligible
sopranos had walked out with Luboš. But he, once the stud of
Nearly Nothing, forsook all others when he realized Heda was
the first woman he would defend with his life.

Everything was planned from the beginning. With enough
off-spring they could form a folk music group. First, fiddlers
were needed. Throughout these pregnancies Heda was subjected
to violin concertos. Next, a cimbalomist was required. She
listened to nothing but piano sonatas for nine months. The
method proved effective. Each child learnt the instrument which
it had heard in the womb. They played as if by instinct, as
if they were born for it, and the family procreated its way to
prosperity.

We sat. Wine was poured. In Bohemia they drink beer so
good it's a wonder that they had a revolution. In Slovakia the
liquor is *slivovice*; the day only begins after a glass of plum
brandy, taken 'to kill the worm'. But in rich Moravia they
make wine so effervescent it is like swallowing something
living.

The family spoiled us but they pampered Ivo. They laid a feast
before him: sweaty smoked salami, marinaded ruby red peppers,
sweet nut-brown mustard and great fists of bread. The crumbs
gathered in the folds of his jumper. Ivo picked at his skin,
checked his fly and grew embarrassed by the attention. But when
the music began the fidgets stopped. He was suddenly still. He
didn't even breathe.

It swept over us like a black heat. The four violins inflamed
the small white room. Clear voices bewitched the space. Luboš's
face, blank when not in song, was transformed. His eyes darted,
conducted, gleamed mica black. Jura, the first violin, taunted
with his fiddle. The strings' whirling demoniacs swirled around
the crisp song. The family sung in one voice with only an octave
between men and women. Heda paused to draw breath. She
must have been eight months pregnant.

'Mother will be better in E major,' instructed Luboš. The
irreverence of Moravian folk music mocked the tragic. 'We sang

this at International Women's Day,' he said and launched into a joyous lilt.

> My wife has died
> I'm a widower.
> They've buried her under a juniper tree.
> Oh three lads have dug the hole
> and they couldn't dig until midnight.
> They have buried her up to her waist
> and here is resting my beauty.

The music stirred something in Vera, not sentimentality but anger.

'I used to imagine', she said, 'that when I'd return to Prague the aeroplane would circle the city. To celebrate my return it would fly a victory roll over Hradčany Castle. But last week, when I finally did arrive, the city was covered by cloud. It cleared only once – over Ruzyně.'

Zita couldn't resist a story. 'The last time I flew with Peter from Moscow I never had such a landing, first one wheel, then the other, we were thrown away more or less. I ended up on the lap of the man sitting next to me. He didn't seem very amused. I wasn't, after all, a spring chicken.'

'I'm not talking about flying, I'm talking about Ruzyně – the prison by the airport. Father had been there too, you may remember. It was almost a family tradition.'

'I don't want you reminiscing all over the place.'

'You knew they were coming for him,' accused Vera.

'Leave that old story at home.'

'You knew.'

Zita was on her feet. 'Oh, shut up. Just shut up.' She looked at the nine doors. 'Which one is the bloody toilet?' It was outside.

The argument had dampened the musicians' spirit. They sat in embroidered frippery and ate spicy sausages, tight in their skins.

'I don't want to be lulled by her lies,' Vera told Ivo.

*

'From uranium we can build socialism' explained away the betrayal. Everyone knew it was a lie. It was all lies. Zita's tragedy was that the lie had become her truth. Fact and fiction were indistinguishable.

'Get me out of here.' Her cry was muffled. Outside under the stars Zita was stuck in the toilet.

'You didn't lock the door, did you?' asked Luboš.

'Of course I locked the bloody door. I didn't want any dicky Tom or Harald walking in on me.'

'The lock hasn't been used since 1968,' he said.

'Well, it works remarkably well.' She shook the door. 'It's bloody dark in here and – *phui!* – it stinks. Get me out.' Winston sniffed at the gap under the door and started to squeal. 'Stop it, Winston,' ordered Zita. 'Mummy's coming.'

'Leave her in there,' suggested Vera.

'That's just the bloody attitude I've come to expect from you.'

'You killed our father,' shouted Vera at the bolted door. Zita kicked back at it.

'Are you completely ga-ga or what?'

'That was unnecessary,' suggested Ivo. Vera ignored him.

'You knew they were coming.'

'I bloody well didn't.'

Ivo tried to smooth the waters. 'Calm down. Both of you. Zita, is the key in the lock?'

'The bastard – excuse me – broke off.'

Vera continued. 'You were a member of the Party. You could have found out.'

'He could have found out. I wasn't even there.'

'It's the wine,' said Luboš philosophically. 'This is always happening.' It was difficult to stay sober in Moravia. He had reached into the ancient lock with a pair of pliers. 'Can you turn the stub of the key?'

'Which way?'

'To your right.'

Vera wouldn't let up. 'You should have warned him.'

'We'll turn the key together.'

'He could have run.' Zita ignored Luboš. 'Why the bloody hell didn't he run away?'

'Because he never believed it would happen to him.'

'Well, it did, like it happened to them all.'

'Zita, turn the key,' ordered Ivo.

'To the left?'

'To the right.'

They twisted together. The old lock snapped in two and fell to the floor. The door opened. The sisters stood face to face.

'I've never killed anything in my life.' Zita's voice didn't rise above a whisper.

'What about the pig?'

'Shh, Winston might hear.' Her cheeks were flushed. 'In any case I didn't pull the trigger.'

On the drive back to town Zita smelt her father. For the first time in years she remembered the naked sweetness of his skin in the morning before he shaved. She recalled the rough scratch of his stubble on her cheek. In the bathroom of black and white tiles she would stand on a chair and plead with him not to drag the flat razor across his face. But no matter how hard she protested he would shave and the warm smell of security became astringent and aloof. She hated the smell which took him away from her, it flooded her nostrils until she could smell nothing else. In the car, in the dark, tears welled in her eyes.

The sisters retired without a word which was difficult as they shared the double sofa bed and inconvenient as we shared the single room. Ivo splashed in the bathroom for hours so, in turn, we stole into the hallway to undress. There were no bedrooms in eastern Europe. Space was so limited that no room could serve a single function. Kitchens doubled as studies, parlours became bedrooms, laundry was washed in bathtubs. I slept on the floor. In the half-light the photographs gleamed like constellations of stars.

The wine lulled us through both the animosity and crows of an insomniac cock. We slept in. The cathedral clock struck twelve which meant it was eleven. In 1645 a confident Swedish general besieging Brno declared he would withdraw his troops had they not succeeded in capturing the city by noon. At eleven, as the Swedes were about to scale the walls, the bell-keeper rang twelve. True to his word the general called off his attack. The bells have rung twelve an hour before noon since that day.

The sisters had headaches. They clasped their heads in their hands and tried to ignore breakfast, chocolate cake prepared by the crone.

'I'm sorry,' said Vera.

'No, I'm sorry,' said Zita. 'Let's collect Mirek and forget everything.' She was conciliatory, maybe because she was trying to bridge the gap between them, or maybe because her spleen had already been vented at another. Ivo had let Winston out during the night and the pig hadn't returned. 'If he doesn't come back I'll wring your bloody throat,' she told her cousin.

We crossed the market and descended the steps into the monastery's crypt. Franz Freiherr lay undisturbed but Mirek's body had vanished. Ascension was unlikely. 'I knew I shouldn't have let him out of my sight,' said Vera and went off in search of a monk.

'That's all we need.' Zita collapsed on the floor against the sarcophagus and lit a cigarette. 'Everything's gone topsy-turvy: blind men collect photographs, the pig's disappeared and now a corpse has walked off. It's unbelievable.'

'The corpse is my husband.' Vera had returned. 'They don't know a thing. The church was locked all night.'

'He can't have gone far,' hoped Ivo.

'They suggested we find the caretaker.'

We dropped deeper into the crypt. Chamber coiled into chamber and down into the catacombs. The remains of the town fathers lay in withered memorial but Mirek was not to be found in the dusty communion. In the darkest corner was a curtain and behind the curtain a door. Vera hammered on its face. There was no where else to knock. 'Open this door,' she demanded. It obeyed. A wizened man in a crisp white smock peered out of the gloom and said, 'Yes.'

'Where is my body?' demanded Vera, surrounded by corpses.

'Your body?'

'My husband's.'

'No body's been interned here since 1784.' He guarded his door jealously.

'We left him here last night.'

'Oh, that body. Is it yours?'

He ushered us into his grotto. Everywhere were boxes and tins. Books were wrapped in newspaper, pens reinserted into their original containers, charts were rolled and returned to cellophane sleeves. Glass jars of grey dust were stacked on every shelf. In the middle of the cell lay Mirek's casket.

'Safe and sound,' he said.

'I thought I'd lost him again,' worried Vera.

'You can't be too careful. Tea?'

Tea was spooned from the box, then replaced in its paper bag. Sugar too was in a sealed pot. Every object was contained within a protective skin. Nothing stood outside its package. Even the broom was wrapped safely in a dust sheet. Our host was the caretaker. He was also an historian.

'A medievalist,' he specified. 'Sugar?'

Once he headed a university department. During the Prague Spring he had written an article on historical continuity. He suggested that the Russian revolution was not a revolt against despotic Czarist rule in general but against the specific reformist Czar. He proposed that Nicholas II's liberal revisions were out of keeping with Russian history, that they went against the grain. The October Revolution toppled the aberrant reformer and Lenin restored the imperialist tradition. Communism was a triumph not of progress but of regression. When the Prague Spring was crushed, the authorities asked the historian to retract his paper. But he believed the words he had written and refused. He would not be demoralized. They destroyed his career.

'I was luckier than most,' he said. 'I continued to work in my discipline.' He swept up the detritus of decay in the tombs of memory.

We drank tea from china cups stored in sawdust. It reminded me of my nephew, the first child born in generations without misaligned ears. He was three years old when his baby brother died. At first the loss didn't seem to affect him but his parents soon noticed, at birthdays and Christmas, that he no longer ripped the wrapping paper off his gifts unable to contain his excitement. Instead he proceeded slowly. He removed the paper, examined the gift and rewrapped it. He could not bear to lose again. He wanted to preserve the moment. So it was with the historian who strove to capture living memory. But the regime moulded memory and called the lies history. Their past was always in flux, its details adjusted to suit immediate political need. Books placed ideology above truth. The disgraced were airbrushed out of photographs. Heroes rose and fell like tin soldiers on the battlefield of a child's toy box. The past was degraded into insignificance, the present became all-consuming and the future an illusory, utopian ideal.

For Winston, who trotted into the room as tea finished, the present was uncomfortable. Around his snout was a slender silver bracelet of flashing blue sapphires and red garnets. Whatever its initial attraction he no longer appreciated its loveliness. It had clamped his mouth shut.

'Swine,' shouted the historian. 'Give it back.' Winston hid behind the casket and tried, pitifully, to squeal. Our host went down on his hands and knees in pursuit.

'Leave him alone,' demanded Zita.

'Not until he gives it back.'

'What on earth is happening?' asked Ivo.

The historian cornered Winston and pulled the bracelet off his snout. 'There.' It was difficult to tell who was more relieved.

'But that's mine,' said Zita.

'It's Mother's,' corrected her older sister.

The family jewels, flushed down toilets after so many tantrums, had been swept by Brno's effluent down the sewer's oldest channel. The larger pieces had come to rest against a medieval iron grate under the monastery. Years later the historian had found them there. He secured them in small cotton envelopes sewn from an old pair of pyjamas. Winston, it transpired, had wandered into the crypt earlier that morning as the historian attempted to identify a jewel. The gleam of the stones had caught the pig's eye. He'd made off with the bracelet but in the chase around the mummies it had slipped and sealed his snout.

The story was told, the mystery solved. Little notes would be written on little cards in fine copper-plate script. Zita didn't ask him to return the heirlooms but he gave her the slender silver bracelet. He slipped it back over the hand which had discarded it. With the blind man and me at the head, the sisters at the feet, we lifted the coffin onto our shoulders and, guided by the historian, carried it out of the crypt into the daylight.

The End of Europe

CZECHOSLOVAKIA STRADDLED A LINE which divided west from east since prehistoric times. The two great European ice caps met at the Morava. The river marked the *limes* or the limit of the Roman Empire. Centurions stared across its water into the unknown dark forests and feared barbarians. From its opposite bank Vandals would swarm on their way to sack Rome. It formed an eastern border of the Holy Roman Empire; Christianity would be severed along its length and two world wars ignite at the fissure of Europe. Here too, give or take a hundred miles, communism confronted capitalism.

In Prague it was said that the Morava, which divided the Czech lands from Slovakia, separated Europe from Asia. Across the river, it was said, men and women do not touch when they dance. Slovak obscenities are based on defecation while Czechs profane fornication. They are not like us, it was said. But no Slovak would have accepted that Europe ends at the Morava. Invariably it ended just a few miles to the east. It was always just down the road.

The Trabant, its engine panting, strained up into the Carpathians, the great horseshoe sweep of mountains which embraces eastern Europe. A queue of Škodas and heavy Soviet lorries trailed behind us. We had left the city where the sewers run with jewels, the blind collect the past and the clocks strike noon at eleven, for Slovakia but had paused at Austerlitz before crossing the Morava. There Zita had developed a headache.

'How do you feel?'

'Lousy.' She had swallowed some aspirin. 'The trouble is it's a terrible sort of roundabout. You take the pills to take the pain away but the pills make you sick. It's a hopeless mix up.'

There had been nothing to see at Austerlitz. No monument recalled the heroism of Archduke Decimus. His deeds were not recorded in any book but consigned to the family memory.

The Battle of Three Emperors was Napoleon's greatest victory. His sixty-eight thousand troops defeated a combined force of ninety thousand Austrians and Russians. The battle had been a tactical masterpiece. It drove the Czar back to Moscow and forced the Habsburgs to suspend hostilities.

Decimus had conspired to deny Napoleon victory. But the Austrian Emperor spurned his advice. Francis the First retorted '*Ohren sind zum Hören*' and, in a fusillade of guffaws, rode nine thousand men to death. Decimus refused to join the suicidal attack on the French right. Instead he led his small corps on a hare-brained assault at the enemy's main force. He had inherited his father's courage but not his brains. The Grande Armée easily overpowered him. '*Feuilles de chou est fou*' mocked the captors. Napoleon had ordered that prisoners and the wounded be bayoneted. It wasn't Decimus's day. But Marshal Soult, a romantic impressed by acts of quixotic heroism, secretly had Decimus escorted home in time for supper. By nightfall, as he finished his *knedlíky* dumplings, the French had counter-attacked and the allied army ceased to exist.

'Slovakia is beautiful but the Communists have left nothing,' said the petrol attendant, his eyes the colour of walnut. Peasants with broad Slav foreheads and high cheek bones squatted in their fields. The men were tired, resigned and bereft of hope. Every woman looked ready to cry. Above them towered heroic statues, poised in defence of the homeland, which portrayed, ironically, the broken people. There had once been little difference between Czechs and Slovaks. Together they had created the first organized states in eastern Europe. But the Magyars, whose horsemen raided as far west as Nîmes and Champagne, divided them in one of the darkest periods of European history. Fascists and Communists deepened the division. Slovakia had never recovered.

In the villages the ubiquitous factory chimney had replaced the steeple as the centre of town. A cement works dusted lime on the road, the houses, a cyclist's hair. Heavy industry belched smoke. Byzantine onion domes deteriorated into red rust.

'I walked this way,' said Zita but I didn't believe her.

At the start of the last war the family had escaped from Brno to Banská Bystrica. Hitler had annexed the Czech lands and it was dangerous for them to stay in Moravia. Slovakia, a puppet state, was an island of prosperity and stability in war-torn Europe. Here at the foot of their mountain they would be safer. But my great-uncle knew Zita, his youngest, would be safest in Switzerland and sent her to Aunt Osyth.

Osyth was not overjoyed to see her niece. She had never forgiven Zita's father for his betrayal and was jealous of the blossoming fourteen-year-old beauty. In any event she had a new husband who was a wealthy banker with wandering hands. History would not be allowed to repeat itself. So while Hitler's *panzers* blitzed westwards across Europe, Zita was packed off back east to Moravia.

She arrived at the family home in Brno to find the family gone. The old housekeeper, terrified more of the neighbours than the Nazis, wouldn't let her stay. She gave her two loaves of *maisbrot*, the precious last sausage and showed her the door. Zita walked for forty-two days across Moravia to Slovakia, travelling at night and sleeping in barns by day.

'I was as filthy as an old cow and I reeked like a Gypsy,' she recalled. 'It wasn't a pretty picture.'

Oto, her brother, was the first to see her. He didn't recognize her. 'Aus dem Weg, Zigeuner!' he had barked. 'It's me, you great oaf,' she replied.

Her arrival distressed her father. Few virgins survived the war intact. He hadn't raised and educated her only to have her violated by a lice-ridden soldier in a hay loft. He had her spirited into the mountains to live among people whom he trusted. She ran errands for the Partisans. Her virginity only just survived the hostilities. The day peace dawned she lost it to her future husband – and to Lenin.

The light was crisp, the air clear and snow still clung to the hills as we drove into Banská Bystrica, the heart of Slovakia. The

fronts of the buildings on the main square were newly painted,
as they were every five years, in preparation for Liberation Day.
Vermilion banners lined the avenues. But behind the façades the
substance crumbled. Zita failed to recognize the house even when
we drew up outside it. Her memory was stuck like a needle
skipping in the groove of a long-playing record. She refused to
remember the building because it was filthy, the stairs because
the paint had peeled and the apartment because the furniture had
been rearranged. It was as if she did not want the memory to
age. The intensity of emotion had frozen it in time. Yet it was
here, in this once grand residence, that she arrived filthy and
smelling after her trek.

The bell was broken and the door unlocked. The apartment
smelt of last year's apples. We followed the sound of Russian
voices through the meandrine rooms, past clutters of unworn
clothes and unmade beds, dusty pianos and photographs of ice
hockey teams. In the thirteenth room, the allegory in Slovak
fairytales for that which is hidden, were Pavel and Marta. She
worked at her sewing machine. He watched two Baltik tele-
visions simultaneously. One provided sound, the other picture
and both were tuned to Moscow.

'The door was open,' apologized Zita.

Pavel leapt up and circled the room in sharp, quick steps as if
he were about to break into a run. He had been expecting us.
Marta hadn't. He'd forgotten to mention our telegram which he
pulled from his pocket.

'Godfathers,' he exclaimed.

'My family,' said Marta and immediately set about preparing
a banquet. Her effort caused Pavel – whose temper was as short
as his stride – to burst into fiery criticism. She basked in his
assault and withdrew smiling under the barrage of insults. They
hadn't had visitors in over twenty years.

'Why my wife cook all this I don't know.' When, remarkably,
he left us alone, Marta shook her head, 'He was once such a man.
Now he only sits watching television and I do all the work.'

'Dinner, please,' Pavel announced as he returned from the
larder with apples, pungent with sweet decay. Marta served
kapustnica, a cabbage stew the colour of paprika, thick with

cumin-spiced sausages and sour cream. I was intrigued by the television. Banská Bystrica lay a hundred and forty miles from the Soviet border, beyond normal broadcast range.

'Áno, áno,' said Pavel. Yes, yes. 'This is very nice.' He laughed. 'I build top aerial on roof, áno? Eleven metres tall. To see Österreichische Rundfunk. For day one, life was wonderful. The world in our house come.' His highly directional antennae picked up Austrian Television. 'Then a great wind from the west comes, áno? Goodbye, Vienna. Hello, Moscow. Fantastické.'

The aerial had been blown 180° in the opposite direction and stuck. The winds had made the precarious mast too dangerous to climb. They were condemned to receive only Soviet television and worse still, only one channel of it, until a favourable wind blew from the east. 'Fantastické, áno?'

Marta leaned across the table with my serving of halušky, potato gnocchi with grated cheese, and whispered, 'You must marry a Slovak; a girl who can make dumplings.'

But Vera had grown weary of the chat. 'We've not come to marry him off. We're here to bury my husband.'

We slept poorly with Winston at our feet and Mirek in the hall leaning against the larder. Woodworms gnawed all night in the panelling behind our heads. There was no heating.

'Breakfast, please,' said Pavel. 'I'm sorry but I must go. What can I do? The system in the world is very bad. We must work.'

The sisters were arranging the funeral. I had the day free and asked to join him.

'I cannot waiting you breakfast, áno?' I made excuses to Marta. She packed a sandwich to tide me over until lunch.

We rode a bus which bent like an accordion. In the school yard Pavel counted from one to five, paused, then counted back again. Boys stood in two ragged lines. One line held foam balls at arm's length. They bobbed up and down five times then rolled the balls to the other line who repeated the action. The numbing routine was varied only by an occasional bounce of the ball. But the boys didn't mind, it was preferable to clearing weeds from railway lines or sweeping the pavement outside their school. This was 'the progressive tradition of physical education founded on a scientific base in the process of developing the socialist principles of physical education'.

In Czechoslovakia no child owned a baseball bat or football boots. There were no class teams. School sport was limited to callisthenics. Children were forbidden either to compete or to excel; individual skills were suppressed. The tall boy was to jump only as far as the short boy and no further. The levelling extended beyond the playground. Physical and academic education were rated equally so the brainy child who could not run was held back. His marks, once averaged, fell. All because he was never told that he was special. Pavel was their gym teacher but once he had been a coach of the Czech national hockey team.

In 1968 half a million soldiers invaded Czechoslovakia. The Party Leader, Alexander Dubček, was kidnapped, drugged and forced to sign the Moscow Protocol. The country was intimidated but it did not capitulate. The Russians needed an excuse to nail the coffin shut. It came several months later. The Czech ice hockey team beat the Soviets at the world championships in Stockholm. Spontaneous celebrations erupted across the country. Czechs and Slovaks rejoiced in Wenceslas Square, the Aeroflot office was burnt out and police stood idly by as Soviet troops were ridiculed by the crowds.

The Kremlin denounced the acts of 'counter-revolution'. The victory undermined the socialist principles of fraternal sport, that is to say the Russians had lost. More Red Army spoil-sports entered Czechoslovakia. Dubček, who had sent a congratulatory telegram to the team, was expelled from post and party. Ten thousand Czech officers were axed, one hundred thousand people fled the country, half a million men and women – like Pavel and Brno's historian – were forced to leave their jobs for manual labour. In the school yard Pavel continued to count from one to five and back again.

Overnight he was denied ambition and the loss of challenge destroyed him. He lost the courage to be curious and retreated into a world of routine and cynicism. The apartment became a place of sanctuary: for the family in 1940, for Pavel and Marta in 1969. Slovakia was a good place to hide.

*

After making arrangements for the next day the sisters had spent the afternoon arguing in the Museum of the Slovak National Uprising, a building shaped like a severed and distorted globe. The collection was undergoing what was euphemistically called 'historical renewal'. The Uprising, a failed attempt to expel the Germans in 1944, occupied the heart of the country's post-war mythology. Its failure and subsequent veneration were acts of blatant hypocrisy. Now the lies were being corrected and display cases had been opened, texts amended, retouched photographs restored. But Vera remained unhappy with the revision – the past remained a matter of interpretation – and she stormed out in a fury. Zita admitted that she couldn't remember. She was having trouble with the facts. Had she actually forgotten or was she simply refusing to accept them?

Marta emerged from the kitchen with supper; smoked pork, sauerkraut and dumplings which were dense like a steamed white loaf. Apricot compote was served with the meat.

'What's truer: memoirs or memories?' Zita was irritated with herself. 'Bloody hell, I know,' she clutched at a straw, 'the phonograph. You know, with those wax cylinders.'

'The Edison,' specified Vera.

'Oto and I used it. We recorded our voices during the war.'

'*Áno*,' confirmed Pavel. 'Where it now is I do not know. I am sorry.'

'It is in the thirteenth room,' said Marta.

'We look, please,' said Pavel.

'But the dinner will get cold.'

Beyond the thirteenth room lay another thirteenth room. The house revealed itself like an onion peeled, layer within layer. It was filled with furniture and cobwebs. We descended into the clutter of ages. Vera found a dusty crystal perfume bottle, over a foot high, in the shape of the Kremlin.

'Not that bloody thing.' After the war a Soviet delegation had called on their father bearing gifts. 'We had to entertain the bastards,' hissed Vera.

'They seemed very nice,' said her sister.

The delegation had come to buy their father's mine. He thanked them and explained that he had no intention of selling.

They suggested that it was in his interest to accept their offer. He was, after all, a German.

Václav objected furiously. His forefathers may have been Austrian but he was a Czech. His family had lived in Moravia for generations.

'They finished dinner,' explained Zita. 'I'd been serving. I knew after dinner you should drink brandy. So I found this old bottle. I filled each glass – those big snifters – full to the brim. My father nearly had a heart attack. His best bloody cognac.'

'It wasn't the brandy.'

'The Russians loved it. They were carried away, eventually, by their drivers. My father had to be carried upstairs.' Václav didn't sell. The mine was requisitioned a year later.

'Here is,' said Pavel.

A stack of grimy canvases, romantic harvest scenes in gilt frames, hid the phonograph. Zita dragged it into the open. It left a trail like a snail in the dust. She unhooked its wooden dome to reveal the finely tooled black and silver works. The great brass horn slipped onto the reproducer head. 'Edison Records Echo All Over the World'. His signature was etched in gold-leaf.

'Where are the cylinders?'

'Behind the curtain,' announced Marta as she brought in our plates.

'Oto looked fearless in his uniform,' said Zita and opened the sleeves of heavy cardboard. The black wax had discoloured to cloudy white but somewhere in their minute grooves slept her brother's voice. She wound the clock-work motor, slipped the first cylinder over the barrel, set the needle and released the brake.

Don Giovanni crackled hollowly up the horn. 'Not bloody Mozart,' objected Zita and removed it. The next cylinder replayed a pious sermon. An English language course followed, 'Does she go to church every morning whilst in Florence? Yes, she goes every morning with Aunt.'

Vera found more cylinders. Zita rewound the spring, replaced the needle and tried again. Edvard Beneš, the President deposed by the Communists, had been recorded as he spoke to the Senate, '. . . Our state is the key to the whole post-war structure of central Europe. If it is touched . . .' The needle skipped. Zita grew exasperated. 'Where the ruddy hell is he?'

'Wenn alle untreu werden, So bleiben wir doch treu . . .' It was Oto. '. . . Daß immer noch auf Erden, Für Euch ein Fähnlein sei.'

'What the bloody hell's that racket?' she demanded.

'Our illustrious brother singing.'

'When all become disloyal, Then we remain loyal, So that always upon this earth, There may be a banner in front of you . . .'

'He always took himself too seriously,' Vera added.

'. . . Be proud I carry the flag, Have no cares I carry the flag, Love me I carry the flag.'

'It doesn't sound anything like him.' Zita turned to Vera. 'What's he singing?' A girl's voice accompanied the song. 'And who's the warbler?'

'It's you, you're singing the SS song together,' she replied. Vera laughed the sort of laugh lovers make when confessing to infidelity. 'A Communist as a fiancé and a fascist for a brother, I don't know how you resolved that one.'

'And bloody you as a sister, that was the bugger in the woodpile. Oto was no fascist. He was an ordinary soldier and handsome to boot.' But it wasn't true.

'Ordinary soldiers didn't volunteer for the SS.' But they did.

'Don't be ridiculous.' Zita's voice was shrill. 'Oto had no choice.' She held her throat as if to strangle herself.

Pavel looked up from his chop. '*Áno.*'

'Eat, please,' announced Pavel shortly after dawn. Marta had been up for hours to bake filo pastry and stuff it with stewed apples. She didn't want us to go hungry during our day in the Tatras. Pavel fretted at the head of the stairs. 'Come, please.' The borrowed car had arrived.

The Volga was as wide as the river. I sat high in the back like a member of the Politburo, the pig on my lap and the sisters at my side. Mirek was strapped to the roof. They wanted him to travel the last leg of his journey in style.

Pavel and Marta sat in front with the driver. In her thick black

coat and woollen cap, she seemed an unlikely Senior Inspector
for Silniční a Mostní Konstrukce, Státní Podnik – the State Enterprise for Road and Bridge Construction. She spoke of her roads
with pride.

'I built this one in 1973. The asphalt is Albanian.' She didn't
rate local materials. 'If only we could get Trinidad tarmac then
we could build something special. It's the best in the world.' She
knew the details of all the industry along her roads. 'Here's our
toilet paper factory.' The car passed a vast works of railway lines
and grimy shattered windows. Scruffy children played with a
puppy by the gates. 'The original machinery was replaced in
1980.'

Pavel had less enthusiasm for the march of industry. 'We are
happy with our cement works. We could have had ball-bearing
factory. *Fantastické.*'

As we climbed, a purple mist of crocuses blanketed the brown
winter grass. The soil became darker, almost black, like the faces
of Gypsies. The lines of hills dissolved into the horizon and the
furthest range became indistinguishable from a bank of clouds.
The Volga berthed outside a tiny Minorite church. Skeletal
crosses, canted at weird angles, stabbed the barren mound like
pins piercing a voodoo doll. News of our arrival had preceded
us and a small curious crowd had gathered. The broad lined faces
of old women stared from under dark head scarfs and whispered.
A journalist, who only months before had worked for the StB,
took photographs. Zita was relieved that she had dressed for the
funeral. A veil was draped from her skunk busby. Her long skirt
was split to the thigh; not particularly respectful but at least it
was black.

'I had the courtesy not to wear red,' she answered Vera's glare,
'or my Party badge.'

Father Raphael read the rites. The blow of a hammer sealed
the coffin, a sudden noise in the silent chapel. An old man, his
tear-stained face unknown to us, carried the flowers upside down
and led the mourners to the grave. The cemetery seemed airless.
The pall-bearers gasped for breath.

Winston, wearing a black bow, trotted off for a rout. Zita
watched him go with mixed emotions. She had come to hate

pigs in these hills. She jabbed me in the ribs and pointed across the uplands.

'That's where I met your uncle.'

Zita's task in the war was to bring food to the partisans. The work bored her. She didn't mind the solitary walk secreting milk and eggs to the mountain hide-outs but all too often her charges were live pigs. The suilline chores heightened her sense of betrayal. She wanted to wear a silk dress and waltz with an officer in Vienna, not drag a pig on a rope up a hill in Slovakia. Oto would have rescued her but he was stationed in Poland and the partisan officers didn't go dancing much after the collapse of the Uprising. Those who hadn't been captured by the Germans tended to contract tuberculosis or freeze to death. The pigs came to represent her sense of injustice. She prayed for salvation.

In the last months of the war Zita was asked to shepherd a particularly stubborn sow into the hills. She coaxed and cajoled it up the narrow alpine paths. Halfway up a steep incline the swine stopped and refused to move. Zita was cold, damp and in no mood for melodramatics. Over her shoulder she carried a satchel full of newly picked crocuses. She thrust it, flowers and all, over the pig's head and started to push.

But the sow, unlike every other pig she had hooded, panicked. It was spring, the earth was slippery and both lost their footing. They rolled, screaming and squealing, crocuses flying, into a gully. Zita was pinned under the beast. She couldn't breathe. She beat its flanks but to no avail. She began to suffocate. A shot rang out and the sow collapsed dead. Zita's last sight before she passed out was of an officer towering above her, a red star on his *shapka*.

The officer, my future uncle, saw below him a radiant beauty, wreathed in flowers, dying under a pig. He holstered his revolver, pushed the carcass aside and noticed that Zita's ears didn't match. He who loved people for their flaws, whose job it was to exploit weakness, lost his heart.

Zita awoke to find herself being kissed; at least, that was the story she told in later life. At the time Peter was giving her artificial respiration. She scrambled away from him. He apologized in fluent Slovak.

'I am sorry. I thought you were being attacked. I thought that the pig was a man.'

Zita was disorientated. 'Where's my sow?' she asked in German.

'I have killed it.' His German was without accent. His eyes were the colour of teak. Zita saw the red star, the Lenin badge, the dead pig and knew her salvation had come. The die was cast and the first arc of the circle of their lives prescribed.

Peter hadn't told me about the Uprising; at least not this uprising. The story he did tell me behind the garden gate was just that – a story. It was not the truth I had now discovered.

Slovakia had been allied with the German Reich. The puppet regime suppressed its people so brutally that there was no need for an occupation army. In late 1943 communists and democrats, with the blessing of Moscow and London, joined forces to form a single resistance movement. The Slovak National Council, a body balanced between political left and right, was appointed to command the uprising and began to concentrate troops and supplies around Banská Bystrica.

Moscow then ordered its independent partisan units to attack Wehrmacht bases, road and rail bridges before the military preparations had been completed. They knew the resistance, caught only partially prepared, would lack the resources for a sustained fight. They succeeded in wrong-footing the uprising.

German forces marched into Slovakia to put down the insurgents. The Council was forced to act but soon they needed help. The Red Army, only eighty miles away over the Carpathians, promised arms, diversionary attacks and an airlift of the Czech Para Brigade, then under Soviet command, into Banská Bystrica. It failed to fulfil every promise. They sent no arms, they refused to allow the Americans to deliver the equipment made ready at Bari and instead of ammunition their Ilyushins flew in agitators, political commissars and Soviet partisan officers, my uncle among them, to ensure the destruction of the last organized defenders of Slovak democracy. Soviet High Command inflicted deliberate and irreparable damage to prevent the Slovaks from freeing themselves. They wanted to be the liberators and by such liberation dominate the republic.

The insurgents fled into the mountains and the Germans razed one hundred villages in reprisal. They executed thousands and burnt their victims alive in lime kilns. The leaders, all fifteen members of an American Military Mission and two Associated Press correspondents were taken to Germany and shot. Both uprising and independence were crushed.

This was the reason Vera had chosen the site for Mirek's final resting place. Every Czech and Slovak knew about betrayal but no one could talk about it. The people had been forced to forget. They feared their memory, if given voice, might unleash demons beyond their control. But history cannot be buried like a body. Only by telling the truth about the past can fears about the future be overcome.

Where does Europe end? If Europe is the courage to defend the rights of man, does the continent end where fear begins? Are its borders fixed or, like the tide, subject to the pull between sun and moon, of inertia and valour? Courage pushes back the curtain of fear.

We lowered Mirek, his journey ended, into the grave.

HUNGARY

Shadows of History

SMOKY HAZELNUT TREES rimmed by cool morning light pirouetted in the breeze. The branches of ancient spruces hung like mourning weeds. Oaks and hornbeams clung to the slopes. At our feet lay a carpet of green inwrought with snow and flecked with scarlet-cupped narcissi. Zita drank the spring as if it were an exotic elixir, giving her life and revitalizing her spirit. As the days grew longer she shed her chrysalis of thick winter coats, she spoke Italian rather than German, whether it was understood or not, and sang to herself.

The road ran downhill and the Trabant, freed of coffin, swept south out of the Carpathians onto the Great Hungarian Plain. The Kopasz mountains fell away. Their final peak, the volcanic Tokaji-Hegy, tapered like the burial mound of an ancient king. In the hills the air was still chilly but below in the valleys the sun warmed the meadows. Ox-bows glittered like twists of silver. A river of viridescent verges, the Tisza, meandered through malachite fields. Beyond the flood plains, below the naked horizon cut from the sky with a diamond, stretched the Danube and the Russian steppe.

The Magyars, a Mongol tribe, had stormed across the steppes into the embrace of the Carpathians. Their horsemen raided deep into the west, ravaged Germany and Italy and buried classical civilization in the Dark Ages. Their enemies prayed, 'A sagittis Hungarorum libera nos domine' – deliver us from the arrows of the Hungarians – and God answered by defeating them at Lechfeld. The vanquished tribe settled on the Central Plain, abandoned their nomadic habits and organized themselves into a state. But in their hearts Magyars remained wanderers. They felt trapped by any borders, especially those which caught them between German and Slav, and the Hungarians, once feared, became fearful.

The vineyards coiled down the hill and around his house. Alajos grasped us in great carpenter's arms and kissed our cheeks. 'Na, Kinder,' he said, though younger than his cousin. 'Ihr seid zuhause.' You are at home. Zita introduced Winston who sat on his haunches and stretched his long back, enjoying the attention and sunlight. Vera was no longer with us. She had left, as suddenly as she had appeared, to stay in Czechoslovakia with her memories.

Alajos stroked his pepper-and-salt bristles with the stubs of his fingers, the tips severed long ago by a power saw, and limped ahead ushering us into his house and Panni's embrace. She wore leis of dried paprika and in her hands were heavy strings of garlic which she flung around our necks like garlands of flowers. Great sacks of cabbages, boxes of oranges and bags of sweet peppers, their skins as translucent as the skins of Klimt's women, were stacked by the door.

'For Sandor's shop,' she chirped. Their second son. 'You haven't heard?' – as if we'd missed it in the press – 'He's opened a grocery with fresh vegetables.'

The house was as colourful as a painter's palette; red plaid curtains, blue twined carpets, a table cloth edged in lace and embroidered with yellow blossoms. Easter eggs, dyed in rainbow colours, dangled from house plants. There was a clock on every wall.

The shelves were crammed with books, stacked at wild angles, like something the earth had thrust up, a geological slice of civilization. A ribbon of the national colours – green, white and red; peppers, garlic and paprika – had been stitched into Alajos's lapel.

'You can live a quiet life.' His brown eyes were shaped like almonds. 'Eat, go to bed and die early.' A cold dinner had been prepared. 'Or you can come to the *Törzsasztal*' – the regulars' table, a sort of informal town forum – 'and learn something.'

It hurt Alajos to hurry but he hurried none the less. Winston trotted happily beside us. Tokaj had been transformed in the few years since my last visit. The little kiosk which once sold only playing cards had grown into a general store. Signs had sprouted above private doorways: tailor, driving school, *Zimmer Frei*.

'Gute Arbeit, ja?' crowed a neighbour at his gate. The fence and walls gleamed newly white. Houses had been painted, front yards cleared and food was in abundance.

I asked Alajos about the *Törzsasztal*. He gestured at the ground.

'Typically you notice nothing. What are we walking on?' Asphalt: here was pavement where before there had been a mud track. 'You remember, it was a disgrace. No one would walk to the *kastély*.' The old manor house. 'Who wanted filthy feet? And the building was a ruin anyway.' His thick black hair had grown grey and his psoriasis, red scaly patches on cheeks and forehead, had spread. 'Through the *Törzsasztal* we bullied the mayor – an old Communist, of course – to pave the path. We worked on him for three years until finally he agreed. It was built. And what happened? A German tourist happened to stroll up it, he happened to see the *kastély*, he happened to be a developer and now the ruin is a hotel. I'll take you for an ice cream tomorrow.'

By nature Alajos was a quiet man. He hadn't always acted. Only recently had he found his tongue. 'My generation has not had one day of peace,' he said. 'Now I am sixty-three years young and there's so little time.'

He pushed open the street door, cast aside a curtain and found the *borozó*, which usually bustled, deserted. Glasses of wine were left half-drunk. A chair lay on its back. Meals were still warm. The bar had been abandoned as mysteriously as the *Marie Celeste*. The town forum had bolted. Alajos looked at his watch, disconcerted.

A waiter appeared, yawned and mopped up a pool of amber liquid. He detached a cigarette butt from his lip. 'They're outside the museum. There's been an accident.'

We ran through dusty baroque streets toward the central square. Complacent hens scattered in our path and their cock crowed indignantly. Outside the museum a crowd had gathered. The air stank of malt.

A fully laden beer truck had taken the corner too quickly and lost its load. Crates had smashed on the cobblestones, beer frothed under tyres, gathered in pools and ran down drains. No one had been injured and an impromptu market had sprung up to sell the unbroken bottles. A barrel was carried off by a publican. Everyone was drunk.

The *Törzsasztal* regulars roared at the sight of Winston who, despite Zita's ineffectual kicks, lapped up then sat in a beery puddle. They shouted at Alajos. 'Opportunities! You said we must seize opportunities. Look at the pig, he knows a good one when he sees it.' Scorn greeted the suggestion to return to the *borozó*. 'Next week,' they replied. 'There's always next week.'

'Once their stomachs are full they act like stupid goats,' said Alajos, ignoring Winston.

'The grass is always better on the other side of the street,' comforted Zita.

On the climb back to the house Alajos seemed smaller. His broad shoulders bent as if against the rain and his head hung as it might to pass through a low door. His whole being had diminished and his spirit seemed to have shrunk.

'I set up the *Törzsasztal* to encourage people to speak their minds,' he sighed, 'but they don't take much of an interest. They still expect the future to come to them on a plate. Now we've pretty new shops, but has anything changed in their heads?' Winston lay down by a wall and fell asleep. I carried him the rest of the way in my arms.

Tokaj's long dry summers and hot autumns produced a copper-coloured wine with a fragrance of lavender but in the cave behind his house, its stone arches thick with mildew and lined with casks, Alajos drank fruit juice. After the war he had been allowed to keep the wine cellar, built by his great-great-grandfather, but their house had been seized. Private property was to be eliminated and the family was permitted to occupy only half their home for which they were obliged to pay rent. The other half of the building was given to a policeman.

'I'd met my new neighbour once. After the war I went back to school to finish my education. You know I wanted to be an engineer. One day – during Latin class – a man appeared at the classroom door and asked for me by name. I stood up. He showed me his identification card – he was AVH, state security

– and ordered, "Follow me." What could I do? I followed. We walked to the police station. He showed me to an empty room. "Wait here," he said and left me for two hours. Then a man I'd never seen before came into the room.

' "Stand up," he demanded. What could I do? "Have you been to the West?" he asked.

' "Yes," I replied. It was true. "In the war I was a prisoner in Belgium."

'The man slapped me hard across the face and said, "You can go." From that moment I was a collaborator. Don't look surprised, most of us were. I was frightened. Fear makes you co-operate.

'Imagine a man standing behind you holding something metal at your head. It might be a pistol, it might be a fountain pen, you can't tell, you can't turn around, you can only look forward. I had four children, a wife and I didn't want to die. I wanted them to live. They gave the policeman half my parent's house. My tormentor slept in my old bedroom. What would you have done?'

Alajos drew a measure of wine into a siphon. 'Eight-year-old Tokaji Aszú, I think you'll like it.' Then he asked, 'Do you know what democracy is? Tradition. The sum of Hungary's experience is thirty-three months: in 1918 for two and a half years and in 1956 for ten days. We have no tradition of democracy here.' He asked Zita, 'Can your car carry heavy burdens?'

She nodded. 'It's carried a pig, a coffin and my sister across half the bloody continent.'

'Then I want to show you something.'

We left Winston to sleep it off under the vines and drove south through fields of maize along the Tisza. The road was lined with poplars and the evening light fell in mosaics across our path. The Trabant rattled past fens of reed and willow. A white stork stepped in the shallows like an elegant ballet dancer, one foot placed before the other with precision, then scooped up a fish with his bright orange bill. In nests a metre across, atop chimneys and telephone poles, the cocks stood sentinel on one leg above broody hens. Sparrows swooped and chattered beneath the tangle of twigs and sticks.

Before us opened a great body of water above which rose a sweep of concrete framed by heroic statues poised in mid-stride and brandishing lightning bolts.

'It was built by hand.' Alajos spread his severed span. 'By Hungarian and German prisoners of war seven years after the war ended.' He looked at us, one eye narrowed in suspicion, the other wide and round in confession. 'I knew.'

'I was working in Tiszalöki. It's not far from here.' He gestured away from the vast dam. 'One of the engineer's wives wanted built-in cupboards. They were popular in Budapest at the time and no functionary's wife could be without them. So I made her a beautiful wardrobe of beech with walnut inlay and she told me about the riot.'

'The fifteen hundred prisoners who built the dam were treated no better than slaves. They lived on water roots and horse flesh: two hundred calories a day.' Zita's smile, meant to be compassionate, was ruined by the absence of teeth. 'The suffering was terrible, yes; but there was a worse crime – the lie.

'This stretch of the river had been sealed off. No one could get near the site. It was isolated from the world. The men had been brought from Kiev at night in sealed cattle cars. Their guards spoke Russian. Their letters to their wives were taken to the Soviet Union to be posted to Hungary. The prisoners thought they were in Russia, as they were supposed to think.

'The war was over and they demanded to be returned home, home to Hungary, not knowing that they were home, here in Hungary, all the time. Permission was refused so they went on strike, four men were killed, another executed but one man broke free.

'One morning on my way to work – I'd nearly finished the cupboards – I found an old friend. We thought he had died at Stalingrad but he'd survived the war. *He* was the prisoner who had escaped from the dam. But he had become lost in the woods and, not knowing how close to home he was, had given up hope. After walking for days he had hung himself from a tree not five miles from his village.' Alajos paused for breath. 'I found his body, hanging, but I walked away. I told no one. I did nothing.'

*

We slept between cotton wedding sheets long stored in scented drawers. Zita dreamt that she lay in a bowl of potpourri, her bed of dried petals made up by convicts in papier mâché masks. Every face wore a painted smile but every eye had been drawn wild.

In the morning Sandor stacked outside our door carrots and cabbages, melons and marrows, fresh from Debrecen market. Winston lay on a goat-skin rug by the *kachelofen*, a glazed tile oven which warmed the house. Nothing would move him, not even breakfast *kifli*, bread rolls like lengths of lead pipe twisted into a crescent, the Hungarian croissant.

'Tempus fugit.' Alajos wore an old tweed jacket and a sombre air. His hair and beard were combed. He held in his arms fifty-six red carnations. 'Are you going to eat all day? Today we remember the Russian soldiers.'

For years Hungarians were forbidden to honour their war dead. They themselves had been the enemy, their country had allied itself with the Germans against the Red Army so only their conquerors could be remembered. The restriction had been lifted in the previous year and for the first time the Hungarians could be commemorated with all the pomp and ceremony once reserved for the Soviets. The Russian dead were pushed out of mind as easily as the Hungarians had been. Alajos had asked the town council, Communists all, if they would troop out to the Soviet war cemetery as they had every other year.

'On no account,' said the council.

'Their sacrifice – the sacrifice of the individual soldiers – must not be forgotten,' he said. 'If you don't go, I will.'

Alajos refused to obliterate the past. He drew no curtain of self-interest over the window of history. He stood apart and, emboldened by a fear of repeating that past, found the courage to remember. Those men who retained the facility to forget disdained his honesty. Fear had made them liars and no one liked to be reminded of his cowardice.

That morning, a local Catholic remembrance day, Alajos and Panni walked alone to the small cemetery. They carried fifty-six red carnations and fifty-six candles, bought at personal expense, for the fifty-six Russians killed. Neighbours who had joined the solemn ceremony in past years whispered 'Here come the Communists' and spat as they passed.

There was no one else at the gravesides. They lit the candles and placed one, with a carnation, before each of the headstones. They stood in silence for a minute then returned home.

Little Kings

A STORK WHEELED above on white arc wings, dipped its long black primary feathers and turned toward a hazy horizon. The road to Budapest bore us south through the Hungary that Zita remembered, the one her grandparents would recognize. Gypsies walked in the dust and bicycles carried workers between farms. Peasants, hoes over their shoulders, returned from orchards. Housewives pedalled home with groceries and paraffin balanced on handlebars. Horses drew carts alongside us, their drivers dozing on beds of reeds. Geese flocked to market, their feathers to fill the pillows of Vienna, and dogs slept in the road, rarely disturbed by traffic. Winston's ears stood to attention like bristled pink envelopes. The sound and scent of his fellows had aroused him. Zita would have enjoyed the company of another pig but there simply wasn't room on the back seat. Winston was growing and liked to stretch his trotters unhindered from armrest to hat box when he snoozed.

The fields unfolded like origami and crossroad towns sprouted beyond the poplars. Nothing, really, had changed on the puszta. The graphite Porsche, racing from Berlin, was a Teutonic knight. Ikarusz buses, stinking of burnt rubber, were stage-coaches. A convoy of Soviet tanks was a Roman century marching to Pannonia. They trooped past an ancient woman whose bowed pegs were wrapped in black stockings and woollen leggings. Neither the march of time nor the thunder of armies – Roman, Ottoman, German and Russian – had ever broken her step. The twentieth century seemed to have been tacked on to the past like an afterthought.

We arrived unannounced in the village of open streams and down a lane of steeply roofed houses, garden gates closed against the world, found Vilmos's folly. The home-made house was wrapped in a skin of pine which had been hewn into onion turrets and mad ornamentation. It had the look of a czarina's summer gazebo, built to quarter scale, and stood out from its neighbours in fantastic, aberrant pretence.

As we stopped, a miniature man, in scale with the building, leapt from a carved chair on the porch. With great ceremony he ushered us into a baroque conservatory, chattering excitedly, and ignored Alajos's letter of introduction. Zita's Hungarian was rusty but she managed to catch the word 'tripe'. A stewed bowl of it stood on the table. A banquet had been prepared, steam rose from the dishes, but the house was empty. We sat on pine thrones, tooled with mazed decoration, while Pappi stroked his elfin ears.

'Can't be for us,' whispered Zita. 'They didn't know we were coming.' We appealed for an explanation. Pappi raised his hand, fingers smeared with wood stain, and begged us to be patient. Then he winked at Zita. 'Tripe gives me the willies,' added my aunt.

The approaching cars made such a racket that Winston hid behind our legs. Three black and green taxis drew up and disgorged a riot of humanity which whooped and whirled into the miniature villa. Pappi grasped his sons, men twice his size, and pushed them through the throng toward us. I was embraced and Zita's hand kissed before our introduction was read. It was the brothers' wedding anniversary. They had married twin sisters thirty-two years ago.

'Willi, not Vilmos,' insisted our host. His moustache was impertinent and he had the shape of head which women wanted to pull to their breasts and stroke. 'And this is József bácsi – uncle Joe – a good man to know.' He deferred to his brother with obvious respect; or was it fear?

'Our parents nick-named me Handsome,' relayed József. I didn't like his eyes and he had a nose that should have had a ring through it. 'Not a surprise, really.' He consciously stroked his lapel, a gesture long associated with Party membership though the Lenin badge was missing, and Zita immediately felt at home.

They swept us into the cyclone and to the table. Five generations clamoured for a place, embraced us, ate. Neighbours arrived, seized vacated seats, ate. Wine was mixed with Coke, glasses raised, 'Hello, hello' went the toast. Behind a screen of carved rosettes great pots cooked on a tiny stove: borsch, spicy *gulyás* and *halpaprikás*, catfish soup swimming on cottage cheese noodles. The tripe was delicious. Pappi bustled cauldrons to the table. 'Grosse Familie,' he crooned in his only words of German and spooned out coils of tripe.

The men, once replete, played cards. Willi dealt. Zita was determined to join in.

'My game may be a little queer,' she volunteered and, laying her hand on the table, said, 'Vingt et un.' They were actually playing skat. Willi reshuffled. Pappi moved from shoulder to shoulder and ground his teeth when wrong cards were played.

'Gin,' she announced out of turn and again laid down her cards. Rules bored her. Poker, bridge, rummy; all were simply card games. Restrictions implied narrow-mindedness. She was profoundly sceptical of formula. She pointed at her cards, 'I've got three nines.'

'How much aeroplane to America?' a neighbour asked me.

'Churchill gave away Transylvania,' declared József. 'Hitler, Stalin, Churchill.' I thought he was being a trifle unfair.

'Stalin was the worst,' interrupted his brother. 'He stuck his nose into every one's pie. That is the correct expression, yes? I must improve my English for business.'

'You don't know your history,' challenged József. 'Look.' He took a modern atlas from the bookshelf. Its first map was historical; Hungary as she was before the Great War. 'This is Hungary. Churchill gave Transylvania to Romania, Burgenland to Austria, Bánát to Yugoslavia. Gone. Our land.' He stabbed the kingdom with his finger. 'This is our land.' In 1918 Austro-Hungary had been divided and dismembered, more than half its territory was given away.

'Churchill had nothing to do with Versailles.'

'We were betrayed. Vae victis.'

'In '56 too,' Willi said to me, 'you – the West – did nothing. You let our children be killed. You left us to dictatorship.'

'That was different,' said József.

'Remember my brother is always right. He is the mayor,' Willi reminded me.

József sat upright. 'And are you still a Party member?' I asked.

'We have our beliefs – and we have our careers,' responded József. 'My brother was in the Party, too.'

'Of course, everyone was.'

'Alajos wasn't.'

Willi sighed. 'Alajos, yes. Alajos isn't a realistic man.' He dismissed him with a wave. 'He didn't do anything.'

'He worried about his children.'

József snorted and Willi answered, 'Worrying about your children became an excuse for doing nothing. The problem was you could never tell if your family was in genuine jeopardy or if you were using it as an alibi for cowardice.'

'He didn't join the Party.'

The mayor burped. 'More fool him.'

'My hobby is no politics,' said Willi. 'But my brother is a politician and he has no choice. I do my woodwork and keep myself to myself.'

'And your taxes from the state.'

'Why should I pay for you to build yourself another villa? How you sleep at night, I do not know. Now I'm a businessman. I run my taxis. Life's become expensive.'

'Ça c'est le problem de l'Ouest,' said Zita, speaking French for no apparent reason other than that it was spring. 'Ça coute chèr, le choix. La liberté n'est pas libre. Qu'est ce qu'ils disent, les Français? Liberté! Egalité! Facteur!'

Willi smiled politely. He hadn't understood a word. 'If only I could afford to live the way my brother lives.'

Willi and József were chancers. As boys they had stuffed fire-crackers into the mouths of frogs. At a Young Pioneers' dinner before the May Day parade they had added laxative powder to the apricot strudel with satisfying results. During the '56 Uprising they were guards on the Austrian border enforcing the false division on Europe. They were too shrewd to tear the red stars from their uniforms and when the tanks returned, inevitable as the cycle of the seasons, the brothers were above suspicion. They seized a profitable opportunity and over the next year spirited hundreds across the border. A little money was made (of course) and it kindled jealousies which threatened to expose them so, at the end of their military service, they moved as far away as possible. In the village of open streams they joined the Party, met twin sisters and married.

While Willi was content to remain a clerk, József pursued ambition. He ingratiated himself with the village council. He said the right words, befriended the right people and was rewarded with power.

'Now they speak behind his back because they fear for their jobs,' said Willi. He polished his brother's ego, always on the point of tarnishing like old silver.

'You do have some honest friends, don't you?' mocked József, 'apart from Alajos.'

'Oh yes, they pay their taxes and don't deal on the black market. They are model citizens and their children are disappointed in them.'

'The kids ask, "Why haven't we got a Mercedes? We've only got this rotten Trabant." Dissatisfaction makes for poor citizens,' expounded the mayor.

'Look at our family.' With a sweep of his hand Willi encompassed the room. 'They went to university, they own cars, my taxis are Mercedes. We have nothing to fear.'

'I arranged his taxi licence.'

'This is my brother and I love him.' They embraced and upset the card table. It didn't matter. Pappi had tuned the radio to a football match. The women retuned it to a music programme. Willi vanished and reappeared playing a battered saxophone. One of the twins, either József's or Willi's wife for we could never tell them apart, followed with an accordion. She glowed like a teenager in love, her eyes glittering almost as brightly as her acrylic jumper. Willi announced that they hadn't played together for twenty years. It seemed an underestimation. The racket was atrocious. The instruments were out of tune and the playing uncoordinated but their enthusiasm was infectious. Everyone was on their feet. Each grasped a partner and whirled around the table. A niece as red-haired as a Celt presented herself to me to be seized. Zita was grabbed by Pappi. He squeezed her bottom when my back was turned. She slapped him but kept dancing. When he squeezed her again a smile broke over her face like a wave on a beach. The tempo increased. The tune was Russian. József broke into a Cossack dance. The family encircled him, clapping and shouting. Their beloved József bácsi dropped lower and lower, spun faster and faster. He moved with an incredible sense of release. He danced until he turned grey and had to be lain on the table like a corpse. Willi simply laughed and laughed. 'Hello, hello.' he toasted. The drink flowed. Night fell.

Zita had never seen the puszta or so she told Pappi when his arm was around her waist. A chorus of disapproval swelled up as if national pride had been offended. The taxis were filled with the trappings of celebration – saxophone, wine, cherry cream cake – and the party transported out on to the plain. Willi, at the wheel of the lead car, roared through the deserted lanes at great speed kicking up clouds of dust. Someone's wife and I were beside him, Zita and Pappi playing the accordion were in the back. The other cars followed.

'Look at it all, all that space,' Willi said to me. 'And we've got a housing problem. It's the Russians' fault, of course. You know they have sixty thousand troops in our country. Well, we offered to drive them home.'

'To Moscow?'

'By taxi. The new government had asked them to leave early – to solve our housing crisis and give us back our barracks. The Russians, well, they apologized. They'd like to help but it was impossible. They had serious transportation problems and it would take them eighteen months to arrange the trains. So we got together – all the taxis in Hungary; from Debrecen, from Györ, from Budapest – and offered to drive them home. The officers, the soldiers, their wives, their children. For free. No charge. But on one condition: that they didn't come back. It was a one-way trip.'

I laughed. 'The offer was no joke. When a division can be moved across the continent in forty-eight hours, why do the Soviets need almost two years to leave Hungary?'

We lurched over a hump and the glove compartment fell open.

Speeding tickets fluttered to the floor. Willi grabbed a handful and tossed them out the window.

'This is why I love democracy.' To commemorate the fall of communism, the authorities had granted amnesty to all traffic offenders. He threw away another handful. 'Goodbye, goodbye.'

The road swept through the grasses like a causeway over the sea. Homesteads were tethered to pontoons, their broad eaves thatched to the ground and washed by verdant waves. Islands of rushes were stacked in conical mounds like camps of wigwams. But soon the camps, the lights and even the acacia trees fell away behind us. A great barren plain, Europe's largest deserted grassland, opened before us.

The silence, when the cars stopped, was deafening. Heaven was an embroidered cloth of stars draped from pole to pole. The earth was flat not round and its empty horizon was unbroken but for the stab of sweep wells, surreal structures like cock-eyed crucifixes.

The party's spark quickly discharged, grounded by the enormity of space. József, too drunk to walk, was laid to rest on a rug on the ground. Only Winston retained the evening's madness, routing wildly in the sandy soil. An owl fluttered off clutching a shrew supper. Willi lit a fire and the group gathered around. Pappi sang a herdsman's lament, unaccompanied, beating the sad rhythm with his foot. The wind caught his voice and carried it into the dark where cattle, grey with wide sweeping horns, stirred.

'The stars are out in full force tonight,' observed my aunt.

'To Hungary!' József had woken, a glass in his hand, and ordered, 'Drink!' He clapped me on the shoulder. 'We are friends. We will forget Churchill.'

'And Stalin?'

'Forget them all.' He gulped his glass, gasped for air and addressed his brother, 'Willi, look.' He held the steppes in his hands. 'Am I so wrong? Nothing has changed here for ten thousand years.' József expected, correctly, that he would be returned to office in the coming election; nothing ever changed for the little kings. He fell backwards in a stupor. Zita and Pappi had dozed off counting stars. The fire burnt down to its embers. We settled into groups, wrapped ourselves in blankets and let go of time. Willi wandered into the darkness. The air of his saxophone drifted on the puszta as sleep overcame us.

We woke to the whisper of wind. A skylark hovered, suspended in space. Dawn, silver lilac, found us cleansed. We felt fresh as after a bath, the dirt washed away. We paused at a farm to buy milk still warm from the cow. Birds flocked around Zita as they might have around St Francis; a gaggle of geese, red-combed hens with chicks, flights of love birds and doves on the terracotta roof. At her feet sparrows fussed and disturbed Winston's slumber. Even a stork descended from her great nest. Zita walked through the fray as if the gathering were the most natural thing on earth.

József had a headache so we drove slowly back to the village of open streams and wasted the morning in indolence. It was early afternoon before Zita and I climbed into the Trabant. The family waved us off. As soon as we pulled away from the czarina's gazebo she started to talk.

'Who was that appalling man in the Trot suit?' she asked.

'Track suit.'

'What?'

'It's a track suit not a trot suit.'

'Are you completely ga-ga? It's Trot, from Trotsky.'

'No, track from trotting.'

'Bloody hell and I thought he was a Communist.'

'He was the mayor.'

'Mayor of what?'

'The village.'

'God help us.'

Zita had said little since our departure from Slovakia. The days spent with Vera seemed to have changed her. Perhaps the sisters had acknowledged their differences, perhaps they had reawoken memories of the past. They had parted without words with a clumsy embrace. But along with Vera had gone Zita's imperious manner. She no longer knew where she stood.

I had left her to her thoughts but whatever she had learnt seemed suddenly to have been forgotten. For a moment she was her old self again; my aunt who denied in order to survive.

'You know all this unfamiliar food has played ruddy havoc with my insides,' she confided, 'but I think the tripe sorted me out, the dancing too. It was about bloody time we fell into clover.' Her mannerisms were a good veneer.

We turned west toward Budapest and dentists. The road followed the main railway line toward the capital. Zita knew the route.

'The Budapest Express,' she reminisced. 'Your uncle and I rode it together many, many times.' When she spoke she waved her hands as if to conjure up secrets never before expressed.

'I thought you hated trains.'

'For heaven's sake, not then, then it was the only way to travel: first class Wagon-Lits. The rhythm of the wheels. Ha ha.' She inhaled deeply on a gut-tearer. 'I forgot those times, you know. It was, oh my God, fifteen, no, twenty years ago – our bloody honeymoon and everything.'

'Zita, you were married in 1946.'

'What the blazes, I can't be that old.'

After her rescue from the sow in Slovakia Zita nourished the seeds of love. The Edison was broken, at least it was after she'd ripped out the leather drive belt, and Peter was invited home to fix it. He succeeded. A speech by Tomás Masaryk, the first president of Czechoslovakia, echoed up the trumpet, she removed it and they kissed clutching the brass horn between them.

Too soon he was recalled to Moscow. He asked her to accompany him as far as the border but no further. She was, after all, the enemy. She arrived wearing a red scarf, good proletarian colours, one might have thought, had the material not been cut from a Nazi flag. Two packs of Lucky Stripe secured them a private compartment. They drank looted champagne and first made love on the last night of the war. In the throes of passion, she cried, 'Your face, I must see your face.' He switched on the light in defiance of blackout restrictions. Outside, a soldier, either drunk or inimical, took a pot shot at the passing train. The window shattered, the bulb blew and in the dark, in a whirlwind of soot and embers, my aunt and uncle were joined. The next morning, when she dismounted and watched the locomotive steam him away into Russia, her skin was as black as an African's but for the silhouette of a hand on the buttock that he had clasped all night.

'I love you I love you I love you,' read the telegram she sent to Dzerzhinski Square. Peter avoided reprimand by explaining the message was code which it was in a way. Nevertheless his superiors, cautious men by necessity, were anxious that their protégé not be led astray. He was transferred from Slovakia and reassigned to Hungary. Zita would have followed him up the Limpopo but she only had to go as far as the Danube. They rode the Budapest Express back and forth, back and forth to the border, no further, until my aunt became someone else.

The Moon Was Young

ZITA HAD NO RELATIONS in the capital but she had given a boa constrictor to Budapest Zoo.

It was a city of curves, of colonnades and crescents: the arc of Nyugati railway station, the camber of Chain Bridge, the river itself which bowed around a mad mock-medieval Parliament building crowned by a Tuscan Renaissance dome. From ancient Castle Hill on the Buda bank of the Danube, Pest was a swirl of houses, uniformly five stories high, encircled by the Elizabeth Ring. Yet for all its soft curves Budapest was not a feminine city, neither a maiden like Prague nor a whore as Berlin; it was too ponderous with no intimate corners and the air, once scented by violets, stunk of automobile exhaust and aggression.

We rode a tram which swayed like a boat down dusty tramways to Marx Square but got off at Engels tér by mistake.

'I could never tell the buggers apart,' admitted Zita.

We pushed through floods of people, through an air of offended hatred, toward the surgery. Luckily it hadn't moved. Zita, who had lost the address, remembered the ornate oak doors and aged *Hochdeutsch* notice, 'Use of the main stairway is forbidden for servants and porters.' There was no mention of pigs.

Inside the offices had changed. The waiting room, once a dark Stygian cell, had acquired carpets and bright walls. Illustrated magazines in a half-dozen languages were on offer. A nurse, whose eyes suggested that dentistry held mysteries of sublime eroticism, took our coats. American Express would do nicely.

Dr Kovács, bald as a coot and with a glass eye, bounced toward us. He remembered Zita and kissed her hand.

'What a transfiguration,' she said.

'Dollars,' he said.

Zita explained, rather unnecessarily, her need. Dr Kovács sucked on his perfect teeth. He had married a dentist. His father was a dentist. His grandfather had been the barber-dentist who extracted an abscessed molar from the mouth of the Greatest Magyar, Count István Széchenyi, father of Buda-pest. Teeth, so to speak, ran in the family.

'Let me check.' Kovács scanned his appointment book. He clicked his tongue. There was nothing available for months and his waiting list was very long.

'Dollars?' I said.

'Tomorrow,' he said.

Zita wanted to see the house, their home for the first ten years of married life. We crossed Octagon Square, with its coffee house façades, and walked up Andrássy toward the park with Winston on his lead, an indignity he ungraciously tolerated. The avenue cut a broad swath through the city from its pompous *Grunderzeit* heart to the lush plane tree-lined villa district where aristocrats and diplomats lived near their clubs and embassies. In her time the street had been renamed after Joseph Stalin. The Andrássys, one of the country's most distinguished families, had ceased to exist. But in time Stalin's name too, like his forty million victims, vanished, banished from memory like a bad dream. The boulevard, the most lovely in Budapest, became the unlyrical Avenue of the Hungarian People's Republic. Its days were numbered and, like countless other street and place names behind the curtain, had reverted to its origins after the revolution. Andrássy Avenue existed again and my guidebook, less than a year old, was out of date. But Zita's books, a row of tattered Baedeker's stacked against the rear window which predated both war and occupation, were current. They had been a gift from her father, it was the last time she had seen him alive, and she had carried them with her on the Pannonia Express to her new life.

Their house on Andrássy Avenue had once been owned by Hungarian Jews, one of the rich and respected families who had transformed the provincial bourgeois town into the largest capital in central Europe. But by the time the Soviets requisitioned the Italianate mansion the owners weren't particularly inconvenienced. The father and six children had died at Auschwitz and a sister had escaped to America. Only one child remained and Peter had allowed him to stay billeted in the coach house and employed as gardener.

'He wasn't much good,' recalled Zita. 'His passion was digging holes. He dug up the periwinkle beds, lovely little blue flowers. Your uncle was livid. What the hell was his name?' Zita stared at the house. 'My God, it's grown.' She pointed through wrought iron railings. 'That's where the nasty clay fountain was.' An ornamental terracotta fountain, all nymphs and flourish, had stood in the front garden. Zita's description made it sound very ugly. On his first day Peter had instructed the gardener to take a sledge hammer to it. His father, ashes on a field in Galicia, had erected the fountain.

'It had to go,' stated my aunt. 'The tree's much more beautiful.' A Golden Rain tree, native to the east, drooped feathery, pinnate leaves over the lawn.

'I was happiest here. In Budapest,' said Zita. Her eyes darkened. 'And most frightened.'

Peter and Zita married shortly after her death. No junior officer, whatever his talent, was permitted to commune with the enemy. Their union could not be hidden and it was pointless to lie to the KGB but one could be judicious with the truth. So Zita, daughter of an Austrian industrialist, died and Zita, niece of a Slovak revolutionary, was born with all her papers in order. She broke with family, country and past for love. She lost a father, brother and sister. In their place her lover, her husband, gave her a new identity, a new 'legend'.

Peter, like others throughout the shattered and starving continent, had been sent to Hungary to ensure the smooth transition to communism. The Yalta Conference had guaranteed free elections but, as the Communists were too unpopular to gain power through the ballot box, coercion was required. First the Red Army refused to withdraw, then the Party allied itself with the interim government. Every day, from within, they demanded more and more power, cutting away elected authority like salami, thin slice after thin slice. Aided by the threat of Russian bayonets, they secured control of the police and Interior

Ministry. Their allies were arrested and their leaderless parties absorbed. Finally the election, fettered by fraud and police terror, was rigged. Within a year or two, the Communists became the government in every country of eastern Europe. It was an effective system.

Peter planted window boxes of pansies and ivy. From his sunny little office filled with geraniums and overlooking Stalin Avenue he advised the AVO, the newly formed security police, on how to break a pluralist state. Six hundred thousand Hungarians were branded enemy sympathizers and deported. The monarchy, which had survived for nine hundred years, was abolished. Church schools were closed. 'Fascist terrorist organizations' such as the Boy Scouts were outlawed. The leader of the majority party, the moderate Smallholder's, was kidnapped by the Red Army, accused of espionage and imprisoned for a decade. The Prime Minister was forced to resign. But the greatest terror was not the late-night knock on the door, though that was dreadful enough, but the fear of it. The threat of arrest by men in bulky suits and felt hats on evidence as tenuous as a neighbour's denunciation made cowards of the brave.

While fear spread like a fungus, Peter and Zita's love blossomed. His position secured them a standard of living denied to the masses. Zita wanted a child but Peter had said, 'We have time.' They were privileged. There was a world to conquer first.

He frequently travelled and she accompanied him to Berlin, to Bucharest, to Vienna, always by train. For a time he worked among the alpine lakes of Carinthia and, like fifty years' newly weds before them, they caught the Maestral sleeper – eight p.m. from Déli station – through the Croatian mountains to make love in the tunnels.

The Red Army had occupied Austria with their British and American allies. The prisoners of war included not only Germans but Hungarians, Romanians, Slovaks and Cossacks who had fought alongside the Nazis. Under the Yalta agreement all Soviet citizens were to be repatriated to the Soviet Union, by force if necessary, where they faced slave labour or death as traitors. But the fifty thousand Cossacks, including eight thousand wives and children, held in Lienz and Oberdrauburg had little to fear. Many were not Soviet nationals but exiles who had emigrated during the Revolution and held foreign passports. They felt safe in British hands.

The Cossacks had been the Czar's last fighting units. Their leaders, Krasnov, Shkuro and Vasiliev, were old anti-Bolshevik White Army generals. Vasiliev was once an officer in the Imperial Guard. During the Revolution Krasnov had led his Don Cossacks against Stalin himself at Tsaritsyn. Now Stalin would have his revenge. It was Peter's task to trap the old men.

But the three Russians were not Soviet citizens. They could not be legally repatriated. Peter engineered a plan at Baden-bei-Wien. The spirit of appeasement was contagious and certain Englishmen were persuaded that the hand-over of the émigrés was a test of good faith. Senior British officers were kept ignorant of the betrayal. Post was intercepted, files destroyed, reports skilfully worded and the identity of the émigrés suppressed. All the White Russians and Cossacks were labelled Soviet and deported en masse to the KGB in Judenburg.

The repatriation was not without incident. Women and children had to be driven at bayonet point into the cattle wagons. Cossacks killed their families and themselves rather than face the *gulags*. But, pleasingly, the Soviet's dirty work was done by British soldiers much as the Nazis had obliged in Banská Bystrica. The old generals were executed at the Lubyanka and Peter, the uncle whom I knew only as a resolute gardener wheeling himself about the beloved garden, won both praise and promotion. I had never known him among men but only as a man in isolation. It was a fine work of deception.

Zita and I walked in silence across the Chain Bridge back to our hotel. The building on Magyar Street had been a luxurious bordello popular with foreigners and aristocrats at the turn of the century. A group of British MPs, guests of the Hungarian government, had once lingered at the establishment and partaken of its services. A large bill ensued which the Parliamentarians refused to honour. They insisted that their philanderings should be paid for by their hosts, thereby creating an unpleasant scandal.

The ladies had long since departed. In the place of their tender diversions a television had been provided. The guests, all in track or Trot suits, sat in the foyer glued to the box and ignored the comings and goings of other guests. Nevertheless Zita took the precaution of smuggling Winston up to our room in a large suitcase. He reacted poorly to his temporary confinement and had to be sedated with a generous measure of *barack*, a breathless apricot *schnapps*.

The racket of the television echoed down the bare corridors to our room. My aunt lay in bed and her bunions ached. We had hardly said a word to each other since supper when she'd told me about Carinthia. I hadn't understood. Zita was not blind but how could she – in her yearning for escape, for richness, for love – have ignored the betrayal of the Cossacks?

Sometimes, if she caught me looking, her confidence would vanish. She would drop her eyes and lower her chin. Her fine features lost their haughty nobility and her round musical German, which normally sang crisp rings around us all, would be mumbled. This was one of those times.

'I didn't believe it because I didn't bloody well see it,' my aunt muttered. Only thirty-one of the fifty thousand Cossacks survived the camps. 'We were happy. The moon was young. How was I to know?'

Our appointment was early the next morning. Zita had brought her bedside alarm clock to ensure we didn't oversleep. It was designed as a labour-saving device. One whispered in Russian the words 'Time, please' and the hour was projected on the ceiling. But the sensor was faulty and in the depths of the night Zita had to shout or clap her hands sharply three or four times to activate the mechanism. Finally dim figures appeared above her and before the projection faded she would burrow in her sheets for her spectacles like a hamster rustling in its cage. She rarely found them in time and the process would be repeated. We tended to get up shortly after the performance no matter what the time.

The dentist made an impression. He took a cast of Zita's gums. 'Would you prefer perfect teeth or the natural look,' he asked. She hesitated, her view of perfection had been undermined over the past weeks. She opted for a slight overlap and the flaws of reality. 'They will be ready tomorrow lunchtime.'

The woman who didn't exist had given a snake to Budapest Zoo. Thirty-four years earlier, Zita had crossed Heroes' Square where victories were celebrated and tragedies mourned, with the boa curled around her neck. The story of the tragedy of the snakes had so moved her that she was determined to give the zoo her most beloved pet. My aunt stepped cautiously for the streets were littered with the detritus of the crushed revolt. The barricades had been breached and girders, strewn in the street to stop the tanks, cleared. Plumes of ashes swirled in dust-devils above burnt-out lorries. Of the colossal statue of Stalin, only his great bronze jackboots remained. His head lay shattered on the cobbles. A T-54 squatted at the corner and Zita got a cinder in her eye.

The Hungarian revolution had begun quietly. A peaceful crowd gathered under a statue of the poet Petőfi. Their numbers swelled and they marched to the Magyar Radio building. The security police opened fire and protest ignited into revolution. Hungarian troops, ordered to subdue the rebels, joined them instead. After six days of fighting a cease-fire was signed. Imre Nagy, the one politician trusted by the people, was appointed premier.

Hungary was free for a week. The one-party system was abolished, censorship ended, the Catholic cardinal reinstated in his palace and peasants returned to their confiscated lands. Nagy announced Hungary's neutrality and terminated its membership of the Warsaw Pact. The next day the Red Army returned with six thousand tanks. They fired on bread queues. The university hospital was shelled with phosphorus. In Rákóczi Square rebels who arrived to hand in their weapons, responding to assurances of immunity, were shot. Young men and women were loaded into cattle trucks and, like the Cossacks a decade before, deported to the Soviet Union.

The zoo director at the time was a nervous man happiest around cages. He had heard the shooting and seen his dying lion handler carried in from the street. It made him anxious for the people of Budapest. He imagined a stray shell striking the com-pound. He saw the animals escape: iguanas on trams, leopards in the parks, crocodiles and alligators in the Danube. It was a horrifying thought. But most of all he dreaded the snakes: rattlers in the ruins, the mamba in Gerbeaud's patisserie. Serpentine ter-ror would paralyse the city. So as men and women with rifles stood up against armour, the little bureaucrat, a quiet *funkcio-náriusok*, executed the snakes one by one. The revolution was crushed and the floor of his office, sodden with venom and slime, ran thick with the carcasses of genus Naja and Dendroaspis.

Zita had spent the days beneath Party headquarters, the only building which remained protected by tanks throughout the uprising. Peter was out of town and when rumours of the rebels' bloody vendettas whispered through the cellars she worried for her animals. She had left them – a bush-baby, seven dogs and Beelzebub the boa – in the big house on Andrássy Avenue. The gardener had promised to feed them but only God knew if he was still alive.

Peter returned from Berlin at the head of a column of tanks. Nagy, safe in the Yugoslav Embassy, was offered political asylum. Peter assured the Yugoslavs of the Soviet's honourable intentions. The Prime Minister would not face charges. The Yugoslavs accepted his guarantee of safe passage. A bus was sent to drive Nagy and his family home but on seeing my uncle they insisted he leave the bus. Again Peter's guarantees were persuasive.

As soon as the small convoy left the compound it was sur-rounded by armoured cars. The Hungarians were driven to Mátyásföld military airport and flown to Romania. Nagy was held captive for a year in Snagov Castle, now a popular picnic spot north of Bucharest. He refused to confess to trumped-up charges. In time the amnesic world forgot about the betrayal and Nagy was returned to Budapest for a show trial. He was con-victed and hanged immediately. For years no one knew even where his body was buried.

Together Zita and I led Winston toward the zoo. 'Actually it wasn't that much of a sacrifice,' she whispered. Her gums ached from the morning's fitting. 'Beelzebub was a lot of bother. I had to breed bloody mice to feed her. The little buggers escaped the night the chief of police came to supper. The stupid man went completely haywire when one ran up his trouser leg. I mean, for heaven's sake, it was only a mouse.' Zita sighed. 'So Peter wasn't too sad to see the back of her.'

Wolves stalked and panthers paced from side to side, their eyes gleaming with the madness of containment. Monkeys screamed tormented cries like tortured children. It wasn't a place for Winston. No animals were allowed in the zoo. A sign at the gate read, 'Animals are not permitted.' We left him on the street outside in the care of a pretzel salesman.

In the palm house, a sultry chamber thick with vegetation, the snakes slumbered. A *Python molorus* lazily tasted the air with its forked tongue. Vipers with evil porcine snouts glared through slimy glass walls. The boa, its skin of burnished enamel, glided from a pool. 'But this isn't Beelzebub.' Zita never forgot a face.

In the office where Beelzebub's predecessors had been slaughtered, the new director broke the sad news. Zita's snake had died in her sleep not two months before, dreaming of mice and rabbit suppers. They'd laid her to rest, like all the animals, in a quiet corner of the Pest cemetery beneath a wilderness of wild roses. The director was surprised at Zita's request to visit the grave. It wasn't marked, he told us, but Zita insisted and he obliged with detailed directions to the site.

The apricots were in bloom. Mourners strolled in the spring sunlight clutching vivid bouquets of gerberas, lilies and carnations. Old women gossiped of husbands long dead and sons who had moved to Australia. They idled up avenues of plane trees, lined with black tombstones inset with red stars, enjoying the day out. Beyond the Party members' marble slabs rose walls of cast concrete. A widow stood in a puddle in her best shoes and, shrouded by the smoke from a caretaker's fire, wept before her husband's ashes. His dust was sealed, as so many others, in cubicles like filing cabinets within the concrete walls, five up by fifty across, each drawer marked by gilt lettering and fresh blooms. *Temetni tudunk* - the terse Magyar phrase translated, 'The one thing we know is how to bury people.'

We followed the zoo director's map past the concrete walls deep into a jungle of acacia trees. The woods opened into a clearing and a plot, crisscrossed by mosaic pavement, was encircled by a new tarmac road. It was our destination; Beelzebub's final resting place.

The bodies of animals had been buried in the forgotten corner for decades. Here also, in 1958, Imre Nagy had been secretly interred, face down. Gardeners tending the tombs of the heroes of the workers' movement dumped the compost and cuttings on his unmarked grave. Rubbish collected and trees took root. The year before our visit Nagy had been rehabilitated and Lot 301 was opened. The refuse was cleared and the Prime Minister buried a second time with full honours.

Zita paid little attention to the resurrection. She'd come to remember her snake, knelt quietly in the long grass some way away from the monument and realized she had forgotten how to pray. Later as we walked away she said, 'You know, I've remembered his name.'

'Whose?'

'Theodor, our gardener, of course. Although he's probably popped off too.'

After the uprising when they left Budapest, Peter had found Theodor a job as a gravedigger. He had always been happiest digging holes. We asked at the gate if he still worked in the cemetery but the clerk shook her head. She'd never heard of Theodor and he wasn't on her records. As we stepped back toward the tram the clerk called after us.

'That name. It's Jewish, isn't it?'

'Of course,' said Zita.

'You won't find any Jews here. Try their cemetery, two hundred metres along the road.'

We tramped down a noisy dead end, the terminus of relics and marble-dusted trams. Powder white masons sanded the faces of old stones in readiness for new inscriptions. Their guard dogs worried Winston. The entrance was under an electricity pylon. There was no office, no flowers, no one. The deserted cemetery was more like a wild wood. Ivy had crept into tombs and cracked the stones. Trees had taken root and rodents settled in the

remains. Brambles had swallowed the grandiose monuments of
the pre-war burghers who had the good fortune to die comfort-
ably, choking on a fishbone or falling under a bus, ignorant of
the horrors their descendants would know. It was an infinitely
sad place, not so much because of the lives lost but because of
the dead forgotten. No one remained to remember the dead and
the past rotted away into oblivion.

In the midst of this rankness, in a barren square, rose a memorial to the dead of the camps. An angle of tablets, each twice
the height of a man, recorded the victims of Ausztria, Oroszorsta
and Auschwitz. Names were chiselled in stone, added in pencil,
in pen, with paint by hand, by shaking angry hands. Across the
desolate space pattered an old man dressed in gardener's overalls.
He carried a plastic bag which read in English, 'Death before
Disco.'

'Theodor,' hailed Zita. The old man stopped, startled, unused
to others in his cemetery. 'It's me.' He lay down the burden and
fixed to his pronounced features a pair of wire-frame spectacles,
extracted from a breast pocket.

'Gnädige Frau,' he deferred.

'You remember.'

He walked toward us and bowed. 'Of course, gnä' Frau, the
ears haven't changed though your teeth were better last time.'

'A lot of me was better. How are you?'

'Worse than yesterday but better than tomorrow.' Pessimism
came naturally to Hungarians. Almost without fail they had
placed their faith in the losers of every war since the sixteenth
century.

'You're still working.'

'Until I die, or next weekend – whichever comes first.'

'You're retiring?'

He shook his head. 'Sad days. My mother.' He pointed back
at the plastic bag, violet and yellow on the grey square. 'She died
on Monday, God bless her.'

'Your mother?'

'Her ashes. It goes from bad to worse. Have you seen the old
house?' Zita was speechless. 'Do you know who's in it now?
Western accountants.' He shook his head in despair, a pessimistic

idealist giving up hope. 'Marx was right: economic conditions do determine things in the end. Follow me, gnä' Frau. It's this way.'

Theodor, carrying his mother, led us back toward the gate. Zita found her tongue.

'Did she suffer long?'

'Longer than most, almost ninety years. My father got out with a reduced sentence. He was the lucky one.'

'But how . . . why is she in a carrier bag?'

'She died a week ago. My sister – we're the only two left – she flew from California for the funeral. Mother's last wish was to have her ashes scattered in the sea. Lilly agreed to throw them in the Pacific. But after the ceremony she was so distressed that she left without them. She realized while flying over the Azores, had a breakdown and forgot who she was. Her doctor put her in an asylum suffering from amnesia.' He held the carrier bag aloft. 'Now what do I do with the old girl? Hungary is a long way from the sea.'

'If only the post was more reliable.'

Theodor introduced us to an ostentatious ivy mausoleum. 'Uncle Benjamin was a baron. There were twenty-eight Jewish barons in Hungary before the Great War. He built the house on Andrássy Avenue.'

'I remember his portrait.'

'Yes, gnä' Frau. You put it in the cellar and the marmot made a nest behind it.' Theodor pulled creeper off the tomb. An ornamental portico collapsed. 'Uncle Benjamin would have known what to do. But not me, I'm just a gravedigger without graves to dig. There are no more Jews left to die – other than me.'

During the last war Hungary embraced National Socialism. The rise of Germany meant an end to the injustice of Versailles. Hitler knew the way to the Magyar heart. He took down the borders and promised them land.

The freedom of the Jews was restricted but, because Hungary retained a measure of independence, their lives were relatively safe. It changed one Sunday in 1944. As the Reich collapsed

Germans occupied Budapest. The Gestapo arrived and the Jews were eliminated. The blue Danube ran red.

Fascism, because it was based on tribe, appealed instinctively to the working class much more than communism ever did. Communist theories of class moved the minds, not the guts, of young intellectuals. They touched Theodor who, like most children from privileged backgrounds, rebelled against his parents' values. He degraded their labours and belittled their achievement. Their accumulation of material wealth was not admirable but exposed a shameful exploitation of the weak. He believed that there could be a better world.

As the Red Army, the vanguard of his belief, swarmed across the plain toward Budapest the Jews who had escaped deportation were force marched to Germany. Those who faltered were shot where they fell. Theodor, Lilly and their mother had evaded the final round-up and hidden in a concealed linen closet in their old house.

Budapest, after Stalingrad and before Berlin, was the major city where the world's two largest armies did battle. The capital, which was little touched until the last months of the war, was destroyed. From their refuge Theodor saw the Russian soldiers in their long heavy coats advance along Andrássy Avenue. His elation was so great that he tied a white handkerchief to a stick and ran into the street. The months of hiding and years of injustice were over. He greeted the soldiers with his only Russian word: 'Jew'. They failed to understand. He was arrested and marched to their captain. Over and over Theodor repeated his one word. The Russian officer heard, understood and cried. He had seen the atrocities in Belorussia and the Ukraine and maybe was himself a Jew. He gave Theodor a food parcel and set him free. Later that day, Mongol soldiers under his command, vandals from Asia like the original Magyars, raped Lilly in the linen closet and afterwards stole the sheets.

But that didn't shake Theodor's conviction. 'The genius of Comrade Stalin sees through all the plans of the war-mongers,' pronounced the school books and he believed it. He imagined a cleaner world where the injustice and horror of the past could never again take root. He laid aside bourgeois values for the sake of the vision ahead. The brutality of individuals need not sully the purity of a philosophy. The Soviets, despite the reign of terror, remained his liberators.

Theodor paused at the temple, a rotting neo–Renaissance pile, to collect a shovel. He gestured back into the wood.

'I was going to scatter mother's ashes around the memorial but it's so cold. There's no one there that she knows.'

'Your father?'

'No, they didn't bother to return the bodies.' He laughed. 'When the order came to assemble at the station, he went early. He hoped to be the first to board the train to find a seat. He was an orderly man.'

The monument's starkness had moved Zita. She said without thinking, 'Someone must be responsible.'

'Oh yes, gnä' Frau, but who? It wasn't my neighbours. They hid Jews from the Nazis. I've heard their stories many times. And it certainly wasn't dear Mrs Póczy who runs the bakery, she wouldn't hurt a fly. She told me that there was someone in the next street but I never met them. So I don't know who is responsible. There seemed to be sufficient fascists during the war but where are they now?'

'Your neighbours didn't see, I mean, they chose not to see.'

'Wouldn't you?'

We had entered a lost lair veiled by thick vegetation. Theodor slashed back the screen of brambles and pushed into a cranny. He started to dig up an anonymous patch.

'I thought it would be safest here. No *funkies* snoop around this cemetery.' *Funkies* were Party functionaries.

A shower of white apple blossoms, blown from an adjoining field, lodged in our hair and on our clothes. Zita stared at the gravedigger, his deepening hole, and wondered what on earth he was doing. Winston happily rootled in the humus. Unlike at the zoo he was welcome here.

'I knew you'd be back for it,' puffed Theodor as excited as a dog unearthing a bone. His shovel hummed like a tuning fork. He hit something metallic. It looked like bronze. 'I'll need some help,' he said.

We scratched away at the trench and using the shovel as a lever up-ended the long protuberance. Theodor brushed it down.

'As requested,' he said.

'What the bloody hell is it?' asked Zita.

Theodor looked crest-fallen. 'Stalin's nose, gnä' Frau,' he replied. Zita sat back heavily on a tombstone.

In that autumn of 1956 the crowd had swarmed to the edge of the parade ground at Heroes' Square. Their objective was the colossal statue of Stalin. A blow torch cut the monolith behind the knees. Students tied cables to a tractor. The tyrant fell and was hacked to pieces by his subjects. His jackboots still clung to the pedestal but the protesters were determined that no trace of the ogre would remain. They climbed up an enormously long ladder carrying saws, hammers and even stones to smash the dictator's feet. Soviet armoured cars arrived to put down the demonstration, tanks circled the plinth, bullets flew, yet the Hungarians continued to hammer the hated symbol of their bondage.

At the height of the shooting, Theodor made off with its conk. Now it was before us, three foot high with nostrils the size of skulls, and he seemed anxious.

'Don't you like it?'

Zita hesitated. A white blossom settled on her nose. 'Very much. Thank you. But what the hell do I do with the bloody thing?'

'Gnädige Frau, when you asked me to steal it for you I assumed that you had a plan.'

'Did I? Well, then I'm sure I did. I often do. Or did. But the plan, whatever it was, seems to have escaped me for the moment.'

'I could lose it until you remember.'

'No, I might be dead by then. It's too large for a doorstop, isn't it?'

'Yes. Too large.'

'We can't take it back to the hotel on the tram.'

'It might start another riot,' Theodor pointed out.

'Could we come back and get it tomorrow? After the dentist we're driving back to Berlin.'

Zita had remained, despite Peter's abhorrence of materialism, a magpie. She loved to surround herself with objects. Their house rattled with alabaster hippos, Palekh lacquer boxes and empty tins of Malossol caviar. Nothing was ever thrown out. Every object needed a home. She could see the bronze proboscis as a firedog.

The nose was heavy. Theodor and I forged ahead leaving Zita to carry the shovel and ashes. As we stowed the bronze in a spare coffin inside the temple, Zita asked Theodor if he had married. He shook his head.

'I spent my life looking after Mother. She was everything.' He clasped the carrier bag to his chest until his knuckles, wrapped around the urn within, turned white. 'I don't know how I can face her death alone.'

Zita thought an evening at the theatre would do her good. She wanted to forget the day. We rode the old Franz Josef underground line accompanied by an orchestra. The minute yellow carriages, which smelt of varnished wood, were crammed with cellos, violas and tubas. At the Opera House stop the musicians pipped us into the crowd. Lace, bows and silk evening dress fluttered out of the tunnel, found a path under the horse-chestnuts, then swirled up spiral stairs to their seats. But beneath the gilt and velvet we found the box office was shut, the performance sold out. A doorman directed us along the Lenin Ring, which paradoxically ran into the Franz Josef Ring, to the National Theatre. By now Zita didn't care what play we saw, her bunions were throbbing, and she only wanted to sit down.

The work was not one of social realism. Those days had passed. Gone were the operas idolizing revolutionaries, gone the pompous monologues on dialectical materialism. Once the state, as sole patron, had defined art. The Party saw culture as part of ideology. It was brought to the masses to glorify the work and ideals of the regime.

Instead we watched a new play; a timid document which was well-meaning but lacked focus. In the old eastern bloc, artists were at sea, inundated with possibilities. For the first time in their lives, many were working without guidelines, thrown back on their own resources. After years of skilful obliqueness they tried to speak plainly but, conditioned to assert only certainties, they drowned in self-expression. It wouldn't have been Winston's cup of tea.

Zita sat in heavy silence and massaged her feet throughout the performance. One of her shoes vanished but I managed to retrieve it during the interval.

Late that night back at the hotel Zita couldn't sleep. 'It was me,' she whispered in horror into the dark. 'I killed the Jews.'

'What are you talking about?'

'In the war.'

'Zita you were nineteen years old.' In all her life she had done nothing more anti-Semitic than butter a ham sandwich.

'No. I did it. I killed them.'

'It was only a play.'

'Not the play, the bloody war. Theodor lost his whole family. I did nothing.'

She would not listen to reason. The after-show brandy had gone to her head. 'You're right,' I said, 'you did kill the Jews.' Her breathing stopped. 'We all did, just like we painted the Sistine Chapel and built Chartres Cathedral. It's a collective responsibility.'

'Oto was in the SS,' my aunt admitted.

The next morning, before the dentist, Zita went to the ABC supermarket. She bought fresh bread, soft cheeses and sweating paprika sausages, their skins mottled by knuckles of fat. Our landlady was persuaded to loan us her kitchen. There Zita fried chicken drumsticks, tossed a walnut and apple salad and brewed a coffee-brown bean soup. She produced a great *strudel*, of cherries, raisins and pastry so thin as to be translucent and packed it in the basket with a litre bottle of sour cherry *schnapps*. It was more food than we could eat in a week.

Her dentures were fitted. We paid in dollars. Zita had teeth again. As we drove toward the cemetery she snapped them like garden shears. She seemed to have reached a decision which, in itself, was worrying.

At the temple Theodor presented Zita with a traditional tiny bouquet of violets. He and I laid the bronze nose across the back seat. Winston looked thoroughly displeased.

'We're driving home,' Zita told Theodor, 'then my nephew's off on his tour and good riddance to him. God knows why but he wants to see Poland. It's en route to Berlin.' Her sense of geography hadn't improved. 'I thought you might like to come along.'

'Me?'

'I've packed a picnic and you could bring your mother.'

'But why?'

'To scatter her ashes beside your father.'

'At Auschwitz?' He seemed incredulous.

'It's not the sea, I know, but it struck me as, well, appropriate. They would be together.' She took a deep breath. 'It would help me, too. You see my brother worked there.'

Theodor stepped forward and hit her with the palm of his hand. Zita didn't move but her teeth fell out. He turned, walked away, turned back and returned to us. 'I'll have to get my shovel first,' he said.

POLAND

Picnic at Auschwitz

RAIN DESCENDS ON POLAND LIKE WAR, suddenly like blitz-krieg, as persistently as a siege. It caught us in Kraków. We dodged the fists of water, great drops which might have bruised a child, and thundered into the Pioneer Milk Bar, shaking off the wet. At the door a soggy beggar slurred his 'Holy Marys'. The paper money didn't rattle when he shook his tin cup. Inflation had rendered coins valueless.

Our waitress, a young woman with sky-blue eyes, wrung her dishcloth hands, raw from washing. Her cheeks had been scalded by the heat of the ovens. We ordered ersatz coffee, tasteless but sweet and hot. She let Winston sit under the table and he devoured a plate of potato dumplings soaked in butter. The pig was putting on weight at a phenomenal rate. Diners slumped over steamy basins of soup and wedges of dark, dense, moist rye loaf. The windows behind them cried with condensation. Outside in Rynek Główny, the largest medieval market square in Europe, a queue floundered as if drowning. The lines for spirits were longer than those for bread and meat. The city was drunk, its streets reeled with alcoholics, for the world's most Christian country still suffered from shock.

'Taxi, Auschwitz?' asked retired men with borrowed cars attempting to supplement their meagre pensions. We declined their services but asked for directions.

'You must have a guide,' insisted one in good German. 'My brother died there.'

'I lost my whole family,' said another in English, claiming advantage through the magnitude of suffering. 'I will take you.' But we went on alone.

Spring had been left behind on the other side of the Carpathians. Our drive north plunged us back into winter. Zita, huddled again in her black coat, wrapped a blanket around herself and Winston, asleep on her lap. Theodor clutched his plastic bag, as if the ashes were his mother's spirit, and shivered. The heating had packed up and no end of tinkering could repair it. Zita blew 'hot potatoes' on my arms to keep out the cold.

The Trabant shuddered down avenues lined with chestnuts. Gentle hills, patterned with parallel strips of medieval fields, rolled up the road to wooded crests of monasteries and châteaux. It was reminiscent of the Loire. Lines of peasants bent over their labours and worked the earth, hoes beating rhythmically, their great pear buttocks turned against the world, too busy to watch its passing. A dead black cat lay at the side of the road, struck down on a blind corner. In a village we coasted past a funeral procession. The wooden cross seemed to propel itself forward. Its broad shaft obscured the slender body of a boy, no older than ten, who carried it. The priest followed, his Bible open, dry under the umbrella held by an unshaven man. Behind the hearse, its driver unable to stifle a yawn, walked the shrouded women, wet and singing hymns for the deceased.

The downs fell away. A depression lay before us, a flat marsh of pine woods whose fleshy bark was so red it felt obscene. The wind moaned through the trees and the forest chattered in a thousand different voices of whispers and sighs. We waited at a railway crossing, as many before had waited, for a train to pass, as many before had passed. I thought of the condemned generation, crushed so tightly into freight wagons that their dead stood rigid beside them like marble pillars without room to fall, and their living, their brief time run out, who smelt the warm familiar scent of life until the stench of the ovens numbed their nostrils. The signpost beyond the tracks read Oświęcim. Zita, an Austrian, an Aryan, a European, took me to Auschwitz.

In all the battles in all the theatres of the Second World War one quarter of the deaths were in Poland. One in ten were killed at Auschwitz concentration camp. The night before Zita had had a dream. She was in her garden, behind the green gate, surrounded by all the family and friends whom she had ever loved. There was her father, her sister, Oto in uniform, Tamina her mother. Peter was beside her, with Karel and Stefan the Romanian propagandist, bellowing gusts of laughter as he did before he became ill. Harald was complaining, as usual, about the animals under his feet. He stepped on the marmot's tail and kicked a dog. The dog bit the cat. The cat clawed Winston which so startled Beelzebub the boa that she spat out the barn owl she'd just swallowed. Decimus the Handsome, in resplendent regimentals, flirted with his grandmothers Cantilena and Contralto. The twins flitted and fluttered under his gaze. Osyth Pomona stood aloof, by herself and next to the clematis.

In their midst appeared a conjuror, a beauty with a mane of raven hair and the gift of magic. To the delight of the guests she made rabbits vanish and playing cards disappear. When Decimus's sabre melted into thin air the twins applauded with glee. The crystal Kremlin, which Vera held in her hands, atomized with a sleight of hand. The guests were delighted. The magician tapped Osyth Pomona's shoulder and, in a twinkling, the Countess was gone. Ernst, her first husband who had been gassed at Passchendaele, cheered. He'd never cared for the old cow. No one would miss her. Then, with a touch, rich Step-uncle Horst melted away. Oh, to inherit his wealth. Everyone Zita liked least conveniently disappeared. The magic of the raven-haired woman was a triumph.

But then Grandfather Valtr vanished and Zita cared very much for Valtr. Vera, Václav and Pavel were taken away too. Ivo was next to fade. Zita respectfully asked for her family back. The conjuror shook her mane: it was not possible. The game had turned serious. Karel, Decimus and his eight daughters vaporized into smoke. The animals followed in one swoop leaving no trace. Harald cursed as he went and Oto stood to attention. Zita watched helplessly as her garden emptied.

Finally only Peter remained. With a caress, as wistful as a lover's troth, he too was turned to dust. No one was left but the unknown woman who smiled sadly, put a finger to her lips and was gone. Zita was alone, alone in her loveless garden.

*

The sign said in five languages, 'Beim Betreten der Ruinen droht Gefahr.' It is dangerous to approach the ruins. Zita, picnic basket in hand, ignored it. She led us to a wood of birches next to Crematorium No. 1.

Auschwitz was smaller than expected. The wall of wire had grown, in the mind's eye, with the magnitude of the crime contained. But Auschwitz II or Birkenau, a mile outside the dirty town, was bigger than imaginable. It was like a city, sprawled over the flat plain, an enormous factory of death. Into its jaws rolled the trainloads of Jews, Poles, Russians and Gypsies. Over the course of the war two million perished within its wire. Six thousand each day, every hour two hundred and fifty souls were incinerated leaving behind only incomprehension and bales of human hair.

We spread a blanket on the grass by the spot where on 16 April 1947 SS-Obersturmbannführer Rudolf Franz Höss, founder and commandant of Auschwitz, had been hanged. The rain had stopped. It was dry under the trees. Zita knelt and unpacked lunch. She laid out soup with matzohs, fried chicken, potato salad and *apfelkuchen*. Winston sat uneasily on his haunches. I recalled a photograph of another picnic. It was 1945, the camp had been liberated and five women peeled potatoes around a fire made from dead men's boots to cook their first real meal in years. Behind them in a copse lay bodies, their anaemic limbs like the tubers of tangled roots. The earth was grey with ashes and cinders. A set of false teeth, obscenely pink, had been ground underfoot. The women, quiet and still, smiled gently for the camera, conditioned by half-remembered holiday snaps. Zita poured the *sekt* champagne, bought from the Pewex dollar shop, raised her glass to Theodor and proposed, 'Your father.'

Winston left his wine in his bowl.

'My brother', Zita confessed, 'looked wonderful in uniform. I was so bloody proud of him.' The SS wore black. Their badge was the death's head. They murdered millions. 'He was a guard over the last summer of the war.' She gestured at a watch-tower. 'He could have stood up there.'

'Watching,' Theodor repeated without emotion. 'Just watching.'

*

I never met Uncle Oto. He died before I was born, aged younger than I am now. In fact, until my first trip to Potsdam, I didn't know he had existed. There was no reason to suspect that I had another uncle. But Zita had taken my hand and, soliciting a promise of eternal secrecy, led me to her bedroom. From a nook behind her dresser mirror she had extracted two photographs; long hidden, much loved. Peter had only recently been confined to the wheelchair and Zita couldn't yet accept that he would never again climb the stairs, knock on her door and surprise her. She still kept the portraits concealed. He had insisted years before on their destruction. Her family album had gone up in smoke and the two pictures, which she had hidden beneath her camisole, were all that remained.

We sat on the bed and drank home-made wine which tasted of blackcurrants. The first photograph had caught Oto, dressed in cotton white, with arms stretched wide to encompass the summer sky. His blond hair was thrown back and his face creased with sun and laughter. It had been taken on the last family holiday before he was sent away to school in Austria. At the Italian lakes, big brother and little sister rowed, swam and planned to change the world. Oto loved wild flowers and would take Zita on expeditions high into the Lombardy hills to seek out undiscovered Alpines among the chestnut groves.

School changed him. Away from the family Oto came under the spell of idealistic young men who claimed to be members of an élite. They said that they were the instruments of a great historical mission. Their romantic authority promised to restore national pride after the humiliation of the Versailles treaty. Oto, like his friends and all but a handful of Austrians, was embittered by the loss of Empire. With the Anschluss, the union of Austria and Germany, he lied about his age and volunteered for the Schutzstaffel. The dragon of shame was slain. Oto embraced the Nazi's deluded mission to become a guardian of Führer and state.

He was a faithful correspondent. He wrote to Zita from Munich after the midnight investiture. At the Feldherrnhalle, on the anniversary of the beer cellar *putsch*, tears came to his eyes when, by the light of torches, thousands of voices repeated the oath in chorus like a prayer. He wrote to her from his barracks, he wrote to her from the camps. Totenkopfverbände units were transferred every three months. He was always on the move. His letters, which chased Zita from Prague to Slovakia, gushed with noble sentiments. He was building the better world that they had dreamt of on Lake Como.

For the second photograph, a formal pose, Oto had worn the black uniform with pride. His blond mop, cropped short and oiled, vanished under the peak cap. But Zita had cut off the cap. After the war rather than burn the print she had scissored away the silver braid, the runic double-S flashes, stripped him of uniform until he was just a face, as any other, without history. Only his eyes suggested something different, something ominous. It wasn't the defiance – he'd retained that – but rather something he lacked: an absence of doubt.

Oto was killed at the end of the last summer of the war. Although he died in the field of battle, he had been transferred away from Auschwitz, Zita could never accept the indignity of his death. There was nothing heroic, no reflection of inner being, in her beloved brother's end, only stupidity.

On her bed clutching her crumbled dreams I saw her frailty for the first time. Before my eyes she seemed to lose her vibrant femininity. Her flesh hung loosely from her bones like a boiled chicken's skin. She was tired. She wanted to sleep long until she forgot.

'I feel like a gargoyle,' she said, 'who fell from Notre Dame. I look like one too.'

I left her and the empty bottle with her pictures. As I stumbled down the stairs I too had only one thought – bed. The wine had gone to my head. I found myself suddenly drunk. Peter took one look at me and despaired.

'Not the blackcurrant?' he asked. I nodded. 'I should have warned you.' He rolled to the bathroom, sat me on the rim of the tub and ignored my protests. 'You are not going to sleep until you sober up.' He filled the sink with water.

I protested. 'I'm tired and I'm going to bed.'

'After half a bottle of that rot you'd never wake up.' Peter put his hand behind my head and plunged my face into the icy water.

I swore when he let me up for air. 'You're not leaving this room until you're sober,' he said and dunked my head again.

It didn't take long. The poisonous effect of the wine paled before the dull ache of my frozen head. Thankfully that was the summer the whole vintage exploded and dripped, red and luscious, through the floorboards and down the walls of the room below. I never drank the home-made wine again. But I kept my promise about the photographs though in later years, as politics changed, they came to be framed and hung, with the rest of the family, in the study.

Auschwitz was first created to eliminate the Polish intelligentsia – the Social Democrats, the Communists, dissident church-men – only later was it dedicated to the mass murder of the Jews. The trains arrived night and day. The travellers had been told that they were being resettled, often to Kiev. They fell out of the closed, packed freight cars and for a moment the world looked wonderful. The sky was so high, so blue. They gasped at the fresh air.

Their possessions were taken. You can claim them later. They were divided: the healthy to the barracks, others follow the queue along the railway line, down the narrow steps into a concrete room. Please undress, you are required to shower. Their clothes were folded neatly at their feet. Two thousand at a time were ushered into a chamber to stand under the shower heads. A star of David was painted on the wall. Only then did they realize the deception and cried out but their screams, deafening within, were unheard without the nail-scratched walls. The prussic acid gas, Zyklon-B, killed in fifteen minutes. Elevators lifted the bodies, still warm to the touch, to the ovens. Their limbs were still supple as if in deep sleep. Gold teeth were removed, women's hair shaved, corpses burnt. A pall of smoke shrouded the world.

Sometimes, though not often, the condemned waited naked in the showers for hours, their bladders and bowels aching. There were acts of sadism, of gross brutality and bestiality. Children were torn from their mothers, taken by the legs and swung against barrack walls. But usually not. The executioners were not dehumanized beasts whose only pleasure was destruction and murder. They were fathers, mothers, sons; my dead uncle, me, you. Their work proceeded calmly and methodically, without haste. The hour-long lunch break was never skipped. The machine of mass execution was manned by normal human beings. They smiled as they interred friars, sent Jews and homosexuals to their deaths. 'Führer, befiehl, wir folgen.' Führer, command, we follow you.

The prisoners selected for slave labour lived, on average, twelve weeks. They were made to sing at disciplinary executions where the condemned were shot with dumdum bullets, their brains splattered into the faces of the men in line. The camp band played on as the survivors marched off to work. As a reward for good conduct the clerical office could issue a pass to the Puff, the Auschwitz brothel. Afterwards a visitor, the musky smell of life on his fingers, might hum a popular camp tango called 'Cremo'. The smoke which rose from behind the ring of poplars didn't come from a brick plant, it was the smoke of their children.

In the SS achievement was worshipped for achievement's sake. It was important how one fought not what one fought. Individuals were relieved of the burden of decision. They became cogs in the wheels of state directed by a single man's will. They were willing prisoners of an ethic without purpose, an ethic which, ostensibly for reasons of political necessity, ordered the committal of crimes and presented them as goals of human technological achievement. The aura of purpose did not only seduce Oto. It turned a million ordinary men and women, the combined strength of Allgemeine and Waffen-SS, into mass murderers.

'I know my duty,' Oto might have said. 'The SS obeys orders.'

When a man dies he doesn't shout 'Victory' or 'God save the King', he cries 'Mama'. In the summer of 1944 almost half a million Hungarian Jews were gassed and burnt at Auschwitz. Theodor's father was among them. Their ashes were scattered on the fields. Their dust rose in the air and blew on the wind into every corner that winds blow. It seeped into the linen closet, it crept into the Reichs Chancellery, it fell on the desks of politicians and priests. Stalin brushed it off the treaty at Yalta. Roosevelt swallowed it with his corn flakes. Churchill mixed it with burnt umber and dabbed it on a canvas. It floats still, today, in the beam of golden sunlight which pierces a gloomy room, the dust of the dead.

Theodor toyed with his food. He couldn't bring himself to eat. 'After the war,' he said, 'my mother continued to wash and iron my father's shirts. She could never get them clean enough. Up until the day you arrived they were stacked, white and spotless, in the linen closet. Do you remember the laundry chute?'

'I remember.'

'My mother would go down to the cellar, into the laundry room where we couldn't hear her and cry. But she forgot about the laundry chute. The sound echoed up, amplified by its metal sides. My sister and I would sit in our rooms and listen to her weep two stories below.'

Theodor stood, the plastic bag 'Death before Disco' in his hand. 'She protected us from death. She drew a curtain over the horror. But when she went last week it tore away the curtain and behind, behind there was nothing, just blackness, a black empty hole.'

He left his shovel and walked away toward the fields. A plough had furrowed black ruts in the soil. The ridges of earth lay belly up like great dead serpents.

'Why her?' he asked no one in particular. 'It's me that you should have taken.'

He scattered his mother to the earth and the wind. His prayers were snatched by the breeze. He let go of the empty bag, it caught a gust and was lifted high into the sky, away, out of sight.

Winston was not happy. His spine, which usually described a graceful arc, was tensed dead straight. He squatted in my place. I tried to move him. He irritated me. His damp snout sniffed at the air. I gave him a shove but he wouldn't budge. For no reason I slapped him once then quickly hit him again. Poor Winston. He ran around in circles but not away. Violent thoughts sprung into my mind: kill the pig, throw myself from a car, plunge a fork into a sleeper's eye. The devil whispered in my ear. Do it. Follow your instincts. I remembered a story of Irish farming sisters. Without provocation they hit their pig with a stick. Its squeals amused them so they struck it again and again. They beat it until it was dead.

I didn't kill Winston. Zita gently laid her hand on my arm and I stopped. She said nothing. Only Winston whimpered. Theodor returned from the field. He picked up his glass and raised it to Zita. 'Your brother,' he responded.

There was an hotel at Auschwitz overlooking the camp and Theodor booked a room. He would return to Budapest in the morning by train, back along the tracks which had once carried his father to death. Zita gave away the picnic – which was untouched – and we drove northwards as the long shadows of evening lulled the land to sleep.

May Day Parody

WHERE IS POLAND? Between Berlin and Moscow there is no natural barrier, no line of hills on which a man can stand and say, 'Here is my country.' The Polish plain, broken only by forests and rivers, runs from the Oder into the steppes of Eurasia. Its borders are ill-defined and hard to defend. Over them stormed raiders and nomads. A small Slavonic tribe, the Polanie, 'people of the open fields', settled the land and gave it their name. On the plain a rich diversity of peoples built an empire which stretched, at its peak in the seventeenth century, from the Baltic to the Black Sea, from the Oder to the gates of Moscow. Its king Jan Sobieski led the armies of his noble republic – for Poland was an elective monarchy – to save Christendom. His winged Hussars lifted the Siege of Vienna. He removed the Turks, the only military power which would have checked the rise of his foes, and, in the process, exhausted his country. Only a century later those he saved neatly plucked Poland from the map of Europe. Prussia melted down her crown jewels, Austria turned her palaces into barracks, Russia destroyed her libraries. The despots of St Petersburg, Vienna and Berlin rewrote history to show Poland didn't exist. The state vanished but the nation lived on.

It was either the alternator or the solenoid, I could never tell them apart, but whichever it was the Trabant gasped like a sow with bronchitis. It strained forward, lights dimming, electrics failing. Zita wanted to stop and look under the bonnet but I sensed that, if we did, we'd never move again. I had learnt that the car had to be driven by instinct or not at all. I had no desire to spend the night by the side of the road fashioning a new condenser from a hair curler.

We inched forward with the motor racing and shuddered over crossroads. It seemed that we might reach our destination but unfortunately we aroused suspicion, though not because of our dimmed lights. Winston had developed a habit of resting his snout on the rear window ledge and watching the world slip away backwards. His demeanour tended to attract attention. A police car drove alongside and, despite our pleas and protests, ordered us to stop. They were disappointed to find nothing unusual, apart from Zita's hat, and left us, settling for a dollar bill for each of their children, stalled in the dark. The battery had lost its charge. Zita couldn't even use the cigarette lighter. But help was at hand. A farmer, off to market, offered to tow us to a garage. We entered the city behind a horse–drawn cart.

In Latin *Varsovia*, in German *Warschau*, Napoleon called it *Varsovie*, Stalin said *Varshava*. The Poles had reclaimed their capital, *Warszawa*. Warsaw stood on the Vistula, at the mid–point of the river's great arc, where a mermaid had told Warsz, a fisherman, that a great city would be built. It rose, was razed and rose again from the ashes like the nation.

The horse trotted through hideous suburbs of fifteen-storey blocks, the tenements of communism, into a pleasing core of broad avenues and leafy neighbourhoods. We unharnessed outside a private garage. 'I have a Masters in Philosophy,' read the sign. 'I can mend your car and we can talk about Hegel.' The mechanic cradled a ginger cat in his arms. I knew more about solenoids than I did about Hegel and thankfully it was too early in the morning to discuss either. So while the mechanic wrestled with uncertainty, we left to find traces of Oto.

We would recognize Anna by the flowers. She would be carrying tulips, she had said. But so it seemed was all of Warsaw. Trams like florid greenhouses disgorged mourners with armfuls of blossoms. It was Sunday and colour washed through Powązki's gates. No stone was without a fresh bloom. It was inevitable that Poles should love cemeteries after so many wars. Nowhere else have the living so many dead.

We broke away from the crowd and walked along the Avenue of the Generals. Iconoclastic slabs of marble bereft of Christianity recalled Communist heroes. There were neither crosses nor flowers here. It was the only deserted corner of the garden.

We found Anna at the butt of the avenue by the memorial to the victims of the camps; a noble cairn of crisp, abstract lines, its pith impaled by a rough strip of concrete, impressed with the footprints of thousands. Here sleeps our history.

'Poland is a boring country.' She was making a point. 'People want to work hard and grow old in peace.' Anna was an architect and a distant relation of Zita's great-uncle who had moved to the partitioned province toward the end of the last century. His scheme to mine iron ore on the Radomska Plain ended in failure. Like Václav, Zita's father, he would have been better advised to stick to precious metals.

'Oto would have fallen for her,' whispered Zita. 'She's his type – a woman well worth arousing.'

'She's a Pole,' I reminded my aunt.

'Oh yes.'

'I don't know why you're here. You should have come ten years ago. There is nothing exciting for foreigners now.' Anna led us past monuments to Katyń and the Soviet-Polish war, past the soaring headstones of the Polish Squadron, to a glade of birch trees. 'Now there is only hard work.' She knelt down and placed the white tulips on an unmarked grave.

'I have the same nightmare at least once a month.' Jacek, publisher of Nowy Świat, New World, was shouting. I could hardly hear him. 'I wake up and I'm still in prison: no Anna, no Solidarity and no New World. It's all been a dream. I tell my cellmates that I dreamt Poland was free and I had become a successful publisher. They roll away and say, "You've been dreaming again, Jacek. Go back to sleep." '

We had come to a jazz club to meet Anna's new husband. A primitive, eclectic ensemble was playing pan-pipes, African drums and an aboriginal horn. An audience of silent aficionados, like beatniks out of time, drank coffee and ate grilled cheese sandwiches served by a matron in a glass booth. It was more reminiscent of a doctor's waiting room than a club.

'*That* was an exciting time. Sure.' Anna yelled across the table.

She hadn't touched her sandwich. 'But it's over now.' Together they had run a small underground press, risking their freedom to print the new wave of sharp young poets and *Animal Farm* in translation.

'Our tradition of resistance,' said Jacek. It had been the same during the Partitions and the Uprising. While Warsaw was under siege a dozen war bulletins appeared every day, chess players published a monthly newsletter and a club of mountain climbers circulated their underground yearbook. Poland thrived in adversity.

'Sure, I look back on those days with nostalgia. All my friends were joined in a common cause. Now we just argue. We've gone our separate ways. Sure it disappoints me, but only when I'm feeling sentimental.'

When martial law was lifted Anna went back to her studies. She had had enough. It was Jacek who had transformed the back room press into a dynamic publishing house and now planned to run for parliament, the Sejm, as a Solidarity candidate. Anna didn't approve.

'Jacek is a poet,' she said as if it excluded him from reality.

'You didn't always say that.' He turned to us, 'Goethe was a privy councillor in Weimar and Havel is a playwright. What's to stop me?'

'Solidarity,' answered Anna. 'We lived through the Nazis, through forty years of communism but Solidarity is going to finish us off in a year.'

'I can't hear you.'

'I mean, we've fought the revolution, now can we have a new refrigerator?'

'A new what?'

'Can't we go somewhere quieter?' she yelled.

A 'Polski Porsche', the nicknamed Polish FIAT, was little better. It made the Trabant seem spacious. Jacek drove us toward Radzymin, a forgotten hamlet on the outskirts of Warsaw. Along the route every house, every factory gate, every blank wall flourished a Polish flag. But their mounts were paired, designed to fly two flags – Polish and Soviet – and half of every pair was empty. In the cellars of every house and factory, behind the portraits of socialist heroes, lay the hammer and sickle – awaiting future developments.

Jacek tried to make himself heard. 'Nowy Świat first published here. I met Anna here. It's a place for miracles but not only for me; here the Red Army was defeated for the first and last time. Radzymin has paid the price of history. I'll show you.'

. Words had always been Jacek's weapon. At school, when the Communist Youth journal rejected him, he started his own newspaper, *Barykada*, named after the Uprising's broadsheet. He saw himself as an undiscovered poet but no one would publish his work. It didn't occur to him that his poetry might be second-rate even when *Barykada*'s circulation peaked at only six copies.

His attempts at self-expression attracted the attention of his *politruk*, the political ideology teacher with whom he shared only mutual hatred. The teacher labelled him 'blacker than the blackest reactionist' and set out to destroy his wild charge. He knew that he would fail the final national examination and lose his university prospects. But Jacek had other plans. For the exam he wrote a paper of unrestrained bombast, praising Lenin and comparing him to God. To all who knew Jacek it was a work of flagrant irony but to the examiners his essay confirmed the value of a progressive socialist education. Jacek won the country's top award.

Doors opened. Jacek was offered a career in television, writing news, twisting fact to suit the fiction. The power of words fascinated him. Yet, spun in the wool of dogma, they failed to influence the public. Every Pole knew that the news was untrue. When martial law was declared, men in uniform appeared on television. As their tanks rolled into the capital, people put their sets on window ledges, facing the street, to let them hear their own lies.

Anna and her first husband were suspicious when Jacek approached their press. No one could be trusted. His reputation as a news writer was known, his poetry was not. But his enthusiasm convinced them of his sincerity. They agreed to print his work in exchange for assistance.

Because of the danger of discovery, every step of the publishing process was diversified. The words you wrote could cost you your life. Paper had to be gathered from separate sources, printed at different locations, bound in secret. Jacek threw himself into the work, confident that soon he would be in print. He collected paper from across Poland and delivered it to the presses, his radio tuned to police frequencies to avoid road-blocks. Near the end of a particularly circuitous journey Jacek drove through a red light. The Milicja stopped him and the paper was found. Jacek explained that he was taking it to be shredded so that it might not fall into subversive hands. The police weren't amused but his television connections saved him. He was let off with a warning.

But his poems didn't appear. Anna always had an excuse: lack of paper or ink or once even running out of type (which was true). As his frustration grew Jacek realized that he could only depend on himself. He needed to find his own press.

He spotted one, surprisingly, in a scrap yard. He knew it might be a trap, a worm to catch a fish, but his need was so great that he took the risk and the machine (a Roneo Alcatel RV3100) then printed a collection of poems which no one wanted to buy. When he was arrested, for it had been a set-up, his story was not believed. No one risked prison to publish sentimental rubbish. The authorities, irritated that their net had hauled only a small fry, refused to try him for political crimes and charged him instead as a common thief. A few months later when martial law was repealed and political prisoners granted amnesty Jacek was not released. He stayed behind bars for another year.

Anna's husband had left her for a job in Austria and she, now with child, no longer had time for both her studies and publishing. Jacek took over, driven by a new hunger which he couldn't explain, and built up the imprint. Quite suddenly restrictions eased and the voices of dissent became the word of authority. The powerless became powerful. Jacek stepped into politics but his past trod on his heels. Dissension, once a virtue, had become a liability.

Radzymin was rotten. Streets were unpaved, drains collapsed, the town hall tumbledown. Families shared condemned hovels without heating or running water. There was no gas. A drunk lay asleep on the steps of the church.

'Do you know, of all places it's Radzymin he wants to represent in the Sejm.' She thought him quite mad.

In the run-up to the first free ballot since before the war Jacek had joined the election committee. Half a century of dictatorship had clouded memories of the democratic process, details were difficult to recall, so posters were printed which explained how to vote: 'Do *not* show your marked ballot paper to the electoral official.' Jacek tramped from door to door in an attempt to dispel the misconceptions. On voting day he sat behind the ballot box, a Solidarity badge on his lapel.

'Tell me, young man,' asked a pensioner, 'how do I vote against the Communists?'

'Just put a cross by the name of your favoured candidate,' Jacek replied.

'But I left my glasses at home.' She handed him her ballot paper. 'Can you please do it for me?' When he refused she criticized his lack of manners. 'They always did it for me.'

Another asked to vote for his bedridden wife, at home with a broken leg. 'I know how she would vote. She'd vote against the Communists.' Jacek explained the procedure. The husband stormed off then returned an hour later carrying his wife on a stretcher.

Later during the count the poll clerk came across a spoiled ballot and berated his neighbours: 'Who did this?'

Radzymin's repute resulted from the miracle of Warsaw, the event Poles were ordered to forget. In the summer of 1920 the Red Army poured west across Poland. The Soviet Bolsheviks saw the country as the bridge over which their revolution would cross to western Europe. The Poles didn't. Lenin was no different from the Czar. On the outskirts of the capital the Polish cavalry sliced through the invaders and surrounded them. Three Soviet armies collapsed and fled.

'Twenty-five years later when the Communists seized power,' Jacek explained, 'the town was made to pay for history. The site of the Soviet defeat had to be obliterated. Shops were closed, construction was forbidden, the people were moved away and soldiers ordered to paint over memorials to the dead. The government was determined that the town would be suffocated. They tried and failed. That's why I chose Radzymin.'

'But they won't let him stand as the Solidarity candidate.'

'They say I'm a Communist. Me,' said Jacek.

'It was that paper he wrote at school.'

'Maybe they just don't like my poetry.'

We stopped outside the only public building, the Party headquarters, which had been closed and converted into an old people's home. Inmates paced its long corridors and slept five to a room. Jacek slipped us into the basement and, like a man rediscovering his childhood train set, uncovered the press. He cleaned the rollers and inked the plate. Soon it was running, spitting sheets of paper over the floor. Anna seemed content to leave the past behind her.

'The room was sound-proofed because of the inmates. To this day only the Mother Superior knows.'

It took a month to produce a book, each page being printed and bound by hand. After every shift the printer had to clean his hands thoroughly, ink under his nails could threaten the whole enterprise. Everywhere lurked the danger of discovery, arrest, imprisonment. As we watched Jacek's furtive movements I had the impression that the war hadn't ended in 1945, that the Poles had fought on through decades of occupation. An élite had lived in luxury while ordinary people slummed in rooms off dark stair wells and survived on turnip soup. There had been no victory and only now, in the last few months, was there finally peace.

A vase of primroses sat on a ledge outside the door, on the table were lilies. The air was fragrant with the smells of freshly cut flowers and cooking. Anna, her child and Jacek lived with her mother near Army Fraternity Square, the 'Square of Four Sads' in the Polish parlance after the sombre statue of four weeping Red soldiers. The Praga flat, across the Vistula from Warsaw, stood near the spot from where, in 1944, the Soviet Army had watched the slaughter of a quarter of a million civilians.

Anna's mother worked evenings at a former ideological training centre recently converted into a disco. The Party, suddenly cut off from official subsidies, had to make money to survive.

As buildings and cars were their only assets, headquarters had been converted into restaurants and the fleets of black Volga limousines transformed into driving schools.

But she had left us *bigos*, a hunter's stew of smoked sausage, game and sauerkraut which, the Poles say, walks into the mouth. 'Little pigeons' or *gołąbki*, cabbage rolls stuffed with rice and mushrooms, had been prepared for Winston. We toasted each other with crystal glasses of cherry juice. After the meal Zita took out her teeth.

'It's the first of May tomorrow,' Jacek said. 'We're having some friends around.'

'This won't amuse Solidarity either.'

'They've no sense of humour. It's our May Day party.'

'You're celebrating May Day?' Zita shook her head in exasperation. 'This is a completely haywire household.' She didn't understand the Poles.

'We never had luck in Poland.' Zita lay in bed stroking Winston. At night he liked to burrow under the sheets and sleep next to her body. Inevitably he would run out of air and panic, thrashing and squealing beneath the covers. I made my litter of cushions on the floor. 'You see, you almost had a Polish cousin.' She paused to give the words their due.

'No one knew. I'd been on the virgin of conception so often that we'd given up hoping, then like a shot out of the blue, I was pregnant.'

On the Moskva Express outside Warsaw after a picnic supper of quail eggs and Georgian champagne Zita leaned over the sink and vomited. Five months earlier on a warm August night she had announced her pregnancy. She chose her moment with the skill of a diva. Peter had been promoted and they had moved away from Budapest to Prague and then in the summer of 1961 on to Berlin where the preparations for the division of the city absorbed him completely.

He was attached to the security department of the Central Committee. On their orders heavy trucks appeared in the eastern sector one Sunday midnight. They unloaded the rolls of barbed wire and concrete posts. Within three hours the western sectors of Berlin were encircled.

Zita made her announcement the same evening. The sudden change in Peter surprised them both. He returned home as soon as the main crossing points had been sealed. During the weeks that followed when concrete breezeblocks replaced the wire his desk was often vacant. He who had shied away from paternity for so many years applied for leave and took his wife home. He was determined that their child would be born in Russia.

The nausea which Zita felt on the train was different from the first weeks' morning sickness. It was violent. Her body, she felt, had suddenly risen up against her. Peter thought it was the food. He wrapped her in blankets, for her flesh was as cold as ice, and went for a hot water bottle. There were none as the Moskva was a Soviet train so he poured a bottle of vodka down the sink and refilled it from the samovar. They held the warm flask to her stomach, helpless in the hands of God. But its comfort did not ease the pain. Her back arched and their dream burst on the crisp white sheets.

'The baby,' she breathed and the lonely whistle of the locomotive cried through the broken night.

Children. It wasn't possible to try again. The doctors advised that it would be dangerous. My aunt and uncle suffered their loss in silence. He channelled the frustration and pain into renewed zeal for his work. Their failure to have a family enflamed his determination to build another larger family. Their dream of a better world would triumph.

Peter and Zita stood at the edge of the crater, facing the void, and their language stumbled. A self-consciousness arose between them and they were fearful that the silence meant their love had failed. In fact the opposite was true. They had reached a point in their marriage when the emotion was greater than their words could express. They stepped into the darkness without a light.

The next morning we went in search of Oto. I parked the Trabant outside the old town on a hill. It was the only way that our departure could be assured. The philosopher's repairs seemed to lack substance. The battery still wouldn't hold a charge. The only certain way to start was to coast down an incline and pop the clutch.

Poland lost the last war. No other nation suffered so much to gain so little. It is forgotten that Germany and Russia divided the country between them. Only with the assurance of Soviet collusion did the Wehrmacht risk an attack on Poland so Stalin was no less responsible for the outbreak of war than Hitler. The last Polish Defence Group surrendered after fighting the two invaders on two fronts. The promised French and British help had failed to materialize.

'We begin where we left off six hundred years ago.' Hitler was determined that the Poles would be reduced to a nation of helots, those not exterminated would survive only as slaves of the new German Empire. Auschwitz liquidated any doubters. But even before its gas chambers were working Stalin had sent one and a half million Poles to the *gulags* of Siberia and Russia's far north. We forget. Like Frederick and Catherine before them, Hitler and Stalin decreed that Poland would cease to exist. Europe was divided into two parts along the line of the Bug. On one side of the river millions of Soviet slaves prayed for liberation by the Wehrmacht while on the other millions of victims of the German concentration camps awaited deliverance by the Red Army.

Had the dictators not quarrelled they could have controlled Europe, divided as it was between them, for decades. But Hitler, like many before him, feared that one day the Slavs would descend on Germany and he broke the non-aggression pact. His assault on Russia, named Barbarossa, defeated him.

By the summer of 1944 Hitler's armies were in retreat. They had been driven back from the gates of Moscow and prepared to withdraw from Warsaw. The Polish Home Army planned uprisings in advance of the Soviets, to speed their passage to Berlin and remind their allies that they were guests in Poland. In July the Red Army's guns could be heard in Warsaw. Russian tanks were in Praga and crossed the Vistula at Magnuszew. Moscow Radio broadcast to the Polish resistance for the Uprising to begin: 'There is not a moment to lose.'

It began in Żoliborz, the *joli bord* of the Vistula. Young men and women armed with stolen weapons took the Germans by surprise. They drove the enemy from their capital. After five years of hunger and darkness Polish flags waved in the sunlight. Warsaw was free. But then, across the river, the Red Army halted its advance.

The German counter-attack began. Stalin, who had promised support, ignored the Poles' pleas for help. The Waffen-SS reclaimed the city block by block. In desperation the British and Americans began air drops of weapons but Warsaw lay at the very limit of their bombers' range. They needed to refuel at Soviet bases. Permission was refused. The Red Army warned that any aircraft crossing its front would be treated as hostile and shot down. So the Luftwaffe's single squadron of a dozen planes took control of the skies and decimated ancient Warsaw.

The Poles fought heroically in the belief that fervour and self-sacrifice would make up for the overwhelming strength of the enemy while the Red Army waited and watched more civilians die than were killed at Hiroshima.

The Home Army held on for sixty-three days, until they were beaten back to Żoliborz. Near the end the Soviets began limited drops of supplies but they used no parachutes and the ammunition which survived the fall was Russian-made, incompatible with the stolen German guns. In the last hours of resistance the Soviets finally responded to the desperate radio calls. The Poles were told to storm toward the river where they would be evacuated by boats under cover of smoke and fire. There was no alternative. But when the fighters reached the shore there was no covering fire, no smoke, no boats. They were mown down by the Germans.

Hitler ordered that the recaptured city be burnt to the ground. Warsaw, beautiful Warsaw, was reduced to a wasteland of corpses and smouldering ruins. Again the Nazis did the Soviets' work. Rokossovsky, the Russian general, said, 'We are responsible for the conduct of the war in Poland. We are the force which will liberate the whole of Poland.' The Soviets wanted to kill national movements throughout eastern Europe. As the national armies would, eventually, turn against the liberators, they had to be eliminated. The liberation of Poland would take place on Soviet terms. Those who might resist communism had been killed. The nation was abandoned by the West.

'On the anniversary of the Uprising,' Anna had said, 'I used to go to the memorial at Powązki; sure, you remember that's where we met. The cemetery would be filled with candles. Every year I put my tulips on a different grave always choosing someone of my own age. At first it was easy, there were so many, but as I grew older it became more difficult. When I reached twenty-five years I could hardly find anyone of that age who had died, and after I turned thirty it was impossible.'

Poles tell a story about the Uprising. Three officers, an Englishman, a Frenchman and a Pole, were flown to Warsaw on a Soviet aircraft. It was impossible to land because of the fighting and the men were asked to parachute. The Englishman hesitated.

'Why are you waiting?' enquired the Russian pilot.

'I have to clear this action with London,' he replied. London radioed that Parliament had to be consulted and asked the Englishman to wait.

The Frenchman hesitated too and again an explanation was demanded. 'First I will drink a glass of wine.' He so enjoyed it that he paused to finish the bottle.

Finally the Pole stepped up to the door and looked down through the clouds at his besieged capital. He hesitated.

'Why are you waiting?' asked the others.

'I don't want to jump,' he replied.

'Then you are a coward,' said the Russian.

The Pole was indignant. 'Me? A coward? I'll show you that I'm no coward.' The Pole took off his parachute and jumped out of the aeroplane.

The betrayal, so typical of eastern Europe's lost century, exerted a macabre fascination on me. Yet the magnitude of the inhumanity made it seem too incredible. Born with a spoon of finest silver in my mouth I wanted to believe that the genocide was actually only a misunderstanding. I imagined that Stalin would recant and that Hitler would emerge from his bunker and apologize, 'So many? I had no idea. I am sorry.' They would shake the hands of their victims and the world would be a better place.

Like my aunt I wanted to believe; and in so believing we made it possible that it might happen again.

We made gods of men and expected them to behave like saints. We surrendered our God-given individuality to follow their flag. 'Be proud I carry the flag, Have no cares I carry the flag, Love me I carry the flag.' We loved them because they freed us from the burden of self; but we feared them because with our surrender of personality they controlled us. 'The Party is the mind, the honour, the conscience of the people.' Lacking the courage to stand alone, we, poor fools, allowed our fear to enslave us.

And what of Oto? The last letter came from the train leaving Auschwitz. It was late summer, he wrote, the willows of Mazovia swirled in the breeze like the skirts of ballerinas lifted up, perhaps, by the fiery whirlwind from the flame throwers. A merry-go-round played on as the city burnt. Gunfire mingled with fairground music. The Uprising wasn't put down by the Wehrmacht, the regular army; instead the SS was assigned the task. Its companies snuffed the life out of the capital. Oto went with them, armed with illusions and a pistol, never to be seen again.

I had heard that at the height of the Uprising an aged aristocrat in a thread-bare silk dressing gown stepped onto his lofty balcony. He carried a watering can in his hand. The heat and dust of battle had dried his plants: dainty sweet peas, pendulous fuchsias and blood-red poppies. With infinite care he dampened their scorched earth. He watched the soil drink deeply and heard its satisfied whisper. An explosion, closer now, rocked the building. Momentarily the old man lost his balance and dislodged a pot, an azalea. It tumbled down toward a passing German patrol. Oto, Zita's brother, might have walked with the soldiers. They might have been singing. Maybe the flower pot fell on his head and killed him, killed him dead.

'Wenn alle untreu werden, So bleiben wir doch treu, Daß immer noch auf Erden, Fur Euch ein Fähnlein sei.' Did he finally doubt ultimate victory as he fell dead?

'I know my duty. I obey orders,' but when he died he cried, 'Mama'. His remains blew in the ruins, a cyclone of ash, and rolled into the dust of all the fearful.

For he was frightened. How else could such behaviour be explained? He feared the unknown and assuaged it with easy certainties. Everything works in Austria and Germany. Signs direct. Trains run on time. Lights at cross-walks are obeyed. But these certainties have not been created for the greater enjoyment of life. They exist for its mindless operation. The adherence to this extraordinary precision keeps the inner anarchy at bay. The Germans' fear is not foreigners, as is the Russians', but that which is within themselves. They are an emotional people. They fear that of which they are capable.

In Warsaw's old Market Square, surrounded by town houses rebuilt after the war, Zita and I considered the balconies. Two guitar players below strummed 'Stranger in Paradise'. One played rhythm, he only knew two chords, the other picked out the tune on a single string. Their music was so discordant that they could conceivably have had nothing to do with each other were they not joined by electric leads to a common amplifier. They never looked at each other, never talked, never smiled even when an officer took his daughter's hand and danced an impromptu jig. The buskers ignored their audience for they were both deaf.

It was May Day. The flat had been transformed for the party. Furniture was stowed away and deiform portraits of Lenin and Marx, their retouched complexions as flawless as their vision, had replaced family pictures. A single table covered with a red cloth stood against the bare white wall. Red carnations were tied with long ribbons of the Polish colours.

The guests arrived dressed as Pioneers in moss-green shirts and red ties. The women wore no make-up and the men's hair was greased. No one kissed, instead they shook hands. Zita wore a black, strapless chiffon evening-dress circa 1959 and tried, rather unsuccessfully, to enter the spirit of the occasion. But the scene was too familiar for her to parody. Winston sported a red collar.

They began with the 'Internationale'. Most sang in Polish. Zita chirped in both German and Russian. I tried to remember the English words.

Arise, ye prisoners of starvation
Arise, ye wretched of the earth
For justice thunders condemnation –
A better world's in birth.

A young woman, an anaesthetist, giggled. She was hushed into silence. Humour did not befit the seriousness of the occasion. A chant followed: 'Red! Red! Red!' We all took up the cry. 'Red! Red! Red!' Then the Young Pioneer song:

One, two, three, Pioneers are we.
We fear not fascists nor their friends –
We fight for liberty.

Astonished passers-by stopped and stared from the pavement. A young man, his angular features sharp as if whittled by a knife, led the self-criticism. He appeared to speak from the heart.

'I doubted the wisdom of Lenin's analysis,' he confessed.

'Shame!' admonished his peers.

'When I was at Pioneer Camp,' admitted another, 'I wore yellow socks instead of red.'

Jacek opened a volume of patriotic poetry by the Soviet 'laureate of the Revolution', Vladimir Mayakowsky. His voice bristled with practised conviction.

Say farewell for ever to the past
we have turned the course of history,
as human beings and communists
we can never be bloodthirsty.

Anna took up the chant. 'Say farewell for ever to the past.'

'We have turned the course of history!' all cried together.

We started to feel quite mad. The poem and chants, the mantras of dogma, were hypnotic. The words moved us though they were quite meaningless. Jacek and Anna, as the rest, felt torn between fear of the past and responsibility for the present. Where are we? What year is it? Has anything changed? Their nightmare had come back to haunt them.

The parody ended; their dance on the grave of communism

was an act of defiance, a celebration of the resilience of the human spirit. Someone tuned the television to Moscow's May Day parade. The angular man was arguing. 'Of course I'm frightened. Look at history: Russia always invades us and every family lost someone in Hitler's camps.'

Jacek and Anna sat drinking North Korean Old and Old ginseng brandy – 'it takes a firm place among the world famous wine and has become the focus of demand'.

'When I was little I once caught three ants and put them into a jar,' Anna said. 'They started to climb out but I shook them down to the bottom. They started to climb again. Every time they tried to escape I shook the jar and down they fell. Finally, after hours, they gave up, it happened quite suddenly. I watched them for a long time but they made no more attempts to get away. The jar stayed outside for days in the rain and sun but the ants just stayed in a circle and twitched their whiskers.'

Jacek shook his head. 'Communism is not a Polish system. We have never accepted it. Never. This is a place for miracles.'

She shrugged and turned to Zita, 'You must go to Częstochowa. It will be the first free mass since the war. That will be a real celebration.'

'The Reds have been replaced by the Blacks,' said Jacek. A priest's cassock was black. Throughout the Partitions, the Nazi and Communist occupations, Poland, as an idea, never ceased to exist. Over the centuries resistance had come to be expressed through the church. Patriotism and piety were synonymous. But with the retreat of enemies, the spirit of resistance became the body politic and, in a society which had been robbed of the balance of ethnic diversity, the church dominated temporal affairs. Catholicism came close to being a state religion and Poland fell under episcopal rule; at least, that was Jacek's fear.

I asked about his plans. 'Same as always. To fight, to fight to lose again. It is our destiny,' he answered. 'But I might write a few lines of poetry along the way.'

'I thought you said it was sentimental.'

'It is; but Poles are great romantics.'

Field of Faith

IN THE GATHERING DUSK we rattled toward Częstochowa. Here it began; here, eleven years before, a lamp first shone; here, into our headlights, stepped a drunk Pole.

'Bloody hell,' snapped Zita. 'I should never have let you drive.' But I had already hit him.

I pulled off the highway and ran back. A war veteran sat where he had fallen, slicking back his ruffled nicotine-stained hair. Home Army medals jangled on his chest. I asked if he was all right.

'Mind your own business. I state employee.'

Who wasn't? I offered my hand.

'Go. No. Wait. You kill me – nearly. You damn well take me home.' I helped him to his feet. He seemed uninjured.

'You stepped right in front of the car.'

'You lie like dog with fleas.' Jerzy, for that was his name, fell into the passenger seat. His nose, bulbous and rosy, dominated his face as if it were its only feature. He stank of wine and mildew but his clothes looked immaculate.

'You cannot get drink in Poland,' he said, 'you can only get drunk.' When he spoke his arms thrashed up and down as if to churn forgotten words from the ether.

'Which way do you live?' I asked.

'So depend where we now.'

'My question exactly,' pronounced Zita who had retreated into the back seat with Winston. She had been navigating until the map blew out of the window.

'We're on the road to Częstochowa,' I said.

'Every road in Poland leading to Częstochowa.'

'The E75,' I specified.

'Thanks to God, a navigator. Drive on, corporal, drive on.'

We drove through empty halogen-lit streets past soulless apartment blocks to the far side of town. Jerzy suggested the accident offered suitable cause for my arrest. 'You know people all over Poland thrown into lorries and driven to dark, cold cells.'

Zita was rather shocked by the thought.

'No food, no water, unlimited sentence,' he said as he directed us into the shadows. 'Only place for nephew.'

A tired palace of origin unknown yawned out of the darkness. Grass grew between its roof tiles. Birds nested under its eaves.

'You live here?'

'Here my son Andrzej work and we sleep. He hero. Prisoners here too.'

The Trabant lurched over pot-holes the size of fox-holes to the back of the palace. We stopped in front of a large, rotting stable. Jerzy rapped a challenge on a door. 'This Ubecja' – the Security Police – 'open up in law.' Somewhere a dog barked. He hushed us, rather unnecessarily. 'Poland is safe country as long you not make too much noise.'

A man with infinitely forgiving eyes opened the door. His face seemed to be made of handfuls of clay, roughly moulded into a vaguely familiar form.

'Papa?' he mouthed but no sound left his mouth, not even a whisper.

'Where I be?' Jerzy asked for him. 'Run down by imperialists. Lucky to be alive.'

'Nothing imperial about me,' lied Zita.

'My boy.' Jerzy introduced his middle-aged son and struggled to remember a word. 'Defender? Yes, defender of family tradition.' Jerzy jingled his medals. 'What do you think? Better later than never, yes?' He unpinned the baubles and fastened them to his son's chest. 'My father fight Czar, I fight Nazis, Andrzej fight Communists. Once, two, three generations,' he announced proudly. 'But Andrzej is real hero, he just from of prison. I burst with water; excuse.' He gestured at us as he pushed toward the toilet. 'Invite for Lenin luncheon meat supper. That teach them lesson.'

The detainees stood in silent rows or lay leaden on the earthen

139

floor. Józef Cyrankiewicz, the Communist Prime Minister, was frozen mid-tirade. Ho Chi Minh wore an inscrutable bronze grin. Stalin and Dzerzhinski, founder of the Cheka, affected the guise of statesmen. Deprived of his plinth Lenin seemed curiously stunted. Like all communist statues they had been removed. They had been blocking the view. The totems of repression were melted down or consigned to dusty sheds and basements. Prospects were improving all over Poland.

Andrzej, keeper of the statues, spoke no English, German or Czech, in fact he didn't speak at all. Zita repeated her dozen words of Polish in no particular order and to no effect. He didn't respond. She leaned back against a bust of Brezhnev and tried to look composed.

'Forty years of socialism and still no toilet paper,' said Jerzy as he re-emerged. He sat at the feet of a band of joyful peasants, hung his coat on a brawny arm and unscrewed the Wyborowa. He poured the vodka and raised his glass in a toast. 'The Red Fleet.' We looked surprised. 'To the bottom.' He drained his glass. 'In Gdańsk I meet Russian sailor. He hate Poles and told so. Nothing the matter, we hate Russians also. He say Russians more strong and hard and fast and then, insult, he say Russians better drinkers.' Jerzy poured another round. 'So my friends and I take him for drinking: pepper vodka, honey vodka, even Żmijówka, vodka marinated by serpent. Of course he not take, he only Russian and he pass under table. So my friends carry him to tattoo maker. And while he dream of virgin in Minsk we tattoo on his chest a damn big Polish eagle. It much money but worth every złoty.' He roared and spilt his vodka. 'We send Communists to the mushrooms.' He poured again. 'You see statues? Andrzej thinking they go to Stalinland.' A proposal for a theme park to communism had been mooted: the haunted Kremlin, Tunnel of Terror, the Gulag Mystery Ride. It was worrying to consider how successful it would be. His son said nothing. 'Oh, no worry about him,' said Jerzy. 'He lose voice.'

He sat us on a camp-bed between book cases filled with well-thumbed, well-read tomes and *samizdat* pamphlets, under a garish portrait of the Pope, beside a photograph of Hitler taking the salute at the German victory parade in Warsaw.

'You German?' he asked. Zita held her tongue. 'You see under podium explosive enough blow devil back to hell.' He jangled one of his medals. Jerzy had helped set the charges. 'We watch, we wait; nothing happen.' At the last moment the man responsible for their detonation had been transferred. 'The devil step off podium, into car and on to big trouble. God work in mysterious ways.'

In Poland it all came down to history. The Germans ruled the world, or so it seemed from Warsaw in 1942. Yet despite the overwhelming odds, the Home Army operated the largest underground force in Europe during the last war. Trains were derailed, bridges blown up and equipment sabotaged.

But every act of resistance provoked massive reprisals. For each German killed, ten, then twenty, then one hundred Poles were executed. Jerzy was arrested. As he had no chance of survival his superiors ordered him to feign madness. In the dank prison cell he began to goose step and bark orders in German. His captors, not used to Poles imitating Nazis, were at a loss what to do. The harder they beat him the louder he ordered obedience to the Führer. The SS could cope with terror, anger, courage, anything but the irrational. Madness upset their certainties. His transfer to an asylum was arranged. Three Home Army men dressed in SS uniforms and speaking with Berlin accents spirited Jerzy out of their hands.

Andrzej served thick cherry jam to stir into tea, a Russian tradition no longer practised there.

'No more jam,' said Jerzy.

A cold supper of bread, cheese and tinned meat was laid before us.

'Ah, Lenin luncheon meat,' he raved and tucked in.

After the war the new Communist government guaranteed amnesty to the Home Army. But the soldiers who came forward were accused of collaborating with the Nazis. Tens of thousands of men and women were interrogated, tortured or murdered. Many were sent to Siberian *gulags*.

'It the worst of prisons,' remembered Jerzy speaking with his mouth full. 'A "Prussian" prison.'

The underground burrowed back into hiding and had

remained buried, living in the shadows, until recent months. Only that morning at a grand ceremony had Jerzy been awarded the medals fifty years after his derring-do.

'When I return home Lenin everywhere: in books, on posters, in papers, Lenin's words, Lenin's life. You could not listen to radio without another serving of canned "Leninismus". In those days no can buy fresh meat. Wise Communists replace cow with tin.' Jerzy held up a can. It read 'meat'. 'As Lenin everywhere, so we told, must be in meat too. So when Andrzej asked at school, "What knowing you about Lenin?", he reply, "My father's afraid to eat him for lunch." It get me six months in Mielęcin.' He roared. 'Lenin have no humour.'

Andrzej was a frail child, raised on stories of his grandfather's struggle against the Okhrana. There was little else to eat. His mother had been shot out of hand on the day the Germans took Nowe Miasto, their town on the Pilica river, two hundred kilometres from Częstochowa, and Jerzy was away with the resistance upholding the tradition of his father and all his fathers before him. The old man's exploits against the Czar's secret police nourished his grandson's sense of history. The child peered over the window ledge, in 1944, and watched five thousand Home Army soldiers march through the town to join the Warsaw Uprising. After years of grey occupation the spectacle marked him. He too wanted to fight for his country but grew up in a state which did not represent the nation; to defend the People's Republic of Poland was to attack the Polish people.

National schizophrenia induced physical infirmity. Andrzej was judged unfit for military service. The reprieve allowed him to follow his passion. He became a history teacher. From the lectern he would read his students the official line, for the past had become the property of the state, then lay the text aside and say, 'This is what I believe in my heart really happened.' His grandfather's memories, stories of their forefathers, were passed on to another generation.

But frustration mounted in him like steam in a boiler. He influenced his students, yet nothing changed. Untruths continued to be printed. He felt as useless as he had when a German officer put the Luger under the soft tendrils of hair on the nape of his mother's neck. He wasn't the stone which started the avalanche but the pebble in its path. History swept him up and rolled on unaffected by his existence.

After the first riots in Gdańsk and the shooting of the protesters, he vowed to change its course. The university, his university, had loaned its main hall to the Milicja. Polish boys in Polish uniforms were to dance the night away the day after their comrades had shot unarmed workers. The betrayal was too insidious. He made a crude bomb, a craft he had learnt well on his grandfather's knee, and blew up the hall. No one was harmed. The building was unoccupied. But Andrzej was arrested and sentenced to death. They asked him to sign a *Weryfikacje*, an assessment of loyalty to the regime, to admit it had all been a terrible mistake. If he didn't, they said, his wife too might go to prison or his son fail his exams. When he refused to sign they took him out of his cell, told him he would be shot but instead marched him to an interrogation. Poles like a good joke. His sentence was commuted to life imprisonment. He was sent to a camp, a copper mine, to dig the metal that cast the statues of Lenin and Marx. Rather than teach the truth the historian hacked out the ore which gave substance to the lie. His lungs filled with dust. In the acrid airless vapours he lost his voice. His term was reduced to twenty-five years, then ten, then it was over. He was released and given a job – though not at the university, the dumb cannot teach – but as a night watchman at the stable.

Zita stared at the Stalinist bust below which Winston dozed. 'I know him,' she said.

'You keep damn quiet about that.' Moczar had once been Minister of the Interior, head of the secret police.

'Mietek Moczar; I met him at a party in Moscow. Peter had just been awarded that bloody Order of Lenin.'

'I knew it,' said Jerzy. 'Lock up the silver, Andrzej.'

'The Pope was in Poland,' she continued.

'Here in Częstochowa.'

'They were blabbering about it. Mietek said he wasn't worried about the visit. He said, "The old dogma's dead." Peter took it more seriously. Then in the middle of the argument, his legs gave out. Just like that. One minute he was making a point with a caviar canapé, the next he was flat on his face. Peter was as surprised as the rest of us. His legs had tingled before but we hadn't given it much thought. It was the blood on his shirt which frightened me – and he had a sudden pain in his heart. Then we realized that the medal's pin hadn't been fastened. When he collapsed Lenin had stabbed him in the chest. Even Mietek laughed, and he had no sense of humour, so Peter's legs were forgotten and the party went on all night. We danced until the sun touched the domes of St Basil's. But it was the beginning and everything; the beginning and the bloody end.' She stood beside the fallen idol. 'At least, I think that's Mietek. Memory plays tricks with me.'

'Oh, is him all right,' said Jerzy. 'Red sins have long shadows.'

'Moscow,' was what she said. 'Bloody Moscow.'

Polish society once had been an association of minorities, a haven for the persecuted. Its people spoke a babble of languages and professed a profusion of faiths. Łódź, Mietek Moczar's home, had been a city of three nations: equally Polish, German and Jewish. The Jews were eliminated during the last war and the Germans deported at its end. Poland became wholly Polish and wholly Catholic, a nation of one language and one religion. But as head of the Security Services, Moczar fanned the embers of intolerance. Repeated anti-Semitic campaigns were mounted even when no significant numbers of Jews remained in the country. He inflamed the fears of imaginary conspiracies.

'If Hitler hadn't solved Poland's Jewish problem,' Zita recalled him saying, 'the Poles would have had to themselves.' The tradition of open-minded patriotism had been cowed into xenophobic nationalism.

'At dawn, I take you to Jasna Góra, if I still awake,' Jerzy had promised. We drove through sleeping streets, the darkness daubed violet with the distant dawn. Already, in the shadows, the devout climbed toward the monastery.

The first rays of sun touched 'the hill of light', Jasna Góra, the nation's holiest shrine. We joined the pilgrims' ascent on foot. Their fortress, a walled bastion of devotion, was trimmed in great streamers of Polish red and Papal yellow. In its teeming passages the faithful wound up toward the high altar and the Black Madonna, a Byzantine ikon darkened with age and scarred by the slash of a Hussite sword. 'Mother of God, Queen of Poland, pray for us.' Her image rose, so legend told, above the decisive battle to enslave royal Poland in the seventeenth century. Cannon balls bounced harmlessly off the monastery walls and the Swedish invaders fled in terror.

Jerzy led us through its crowded churches and chapels, their walls adorned with rosaries, necklaces and sacred hearts. The devout offered them up, with their lives, for their nation and their faith. 'Mary, Queen of Poland, I am with you, I remember, I am on the alert.' Everywhere they prayed, out loud or in inward whispers, and without psalters or prayer books for the words were all known by heart. An old man held a sacred triptych carried from home, an old woman bent down in the cool morning sun and cried. Eyes, all eyes, were cast up.

The fields around, where up to a million pilgrims could assemble, stepped down in tiers, the gods, the circle, the stalls, like a theatre turned inside out, and fell away to the town of plane tree avenues which, as rivers to the sea, channelled floods of people to the citadel. At the end of one avenue, beyond the Soviet War Memorial, arose a single provocative chimney in irreligious alignment.

A star-fish building with three wings, the so-called Bermuda Triangle because those who entered it were never seen again, crouched at the foot of the great hill. From here the security police bugged every chapel and alcove of Jasna Góra to keep a tab on the Church. But the building in the shadow of the Lord was now closed.

'Your friendly Moczar lost,' said Jerzy. He fought to find a word. 'Triumph? Yes, that is good word; triumph of Solidarity is triumph for Church.'

On the hill above, at the podium, gathered Home Army veterans and Milicja officers, adversaries reconciled, at the first free mass since before the war. Ribbons of colour, of nation and church, rose in the breeze. The archbishop in resplendent robes led the prayers. The Poles bowed their heads, not in fear but out of love, and sank to their knees on the warm spring grass.

Here it began. Here was the turning point. Here on his first visit in 1979 the Pope broke through the barrier of fear. 'Mary, Queen of Poland, I am close to you, I remember you, I watch.' For nine extraordinary days millions turned out to follow him, listen to him and pray with him. The People's Republic, the political cadaver, ceased to exist except as the censor of television coverage. 'What does it mean, "I watch"? It means that I make an effort to be a person of conscience. I do not stifle this conscience and I do not deform it. I call good and evil by name.' The Pope declared that their future would depend on those mature enough to be non-conformists, then asked them to conform with the Church. The gentle crowd stood together against the Party-state; in a year Solidarity was born, in ten years the Berlin Wall would fall.

John Paul II picked up a small girl and asked her, 'Where is Poland?' She stared at him, bewildered. He placed his hand gently over her heart and said, 'Poland is here.'

God placed Poland at the heart of Europe. But, as with man, He missed. Our heart lies off-centre, on the wrong side of Germany. The Polish nation, the eastern-most bulwark of Latin Christendom, should nestle next to France or be moored to Britain, not lie trapped, as it is, on the open plains between two hungry autocracies where its democracy clashed with its neighbour's despotism, its individualism with their collectivism, its Catholicism with Russian Orthodoxy and German Protestantism.

'At end of war,' said Jerzy, 'Stalin taking over from God. He moving Poland west one hundred fifty mile and stealing many land. For once old butcher not going enough far. Why he not pushing us right across Rhine into better neighbourhood?'

There being no spare beds in the stable, Jerzy passed us on to friends. We lay down in a tidy farm house of three low rooms under a photograph of the Pope. That night Zita slept so deeply that when she awoke her face was washed smooth as if the dirt of years had been swept away by a flood. Her cherished certainties, built on sand, were crumbling into the tide. I too thought I heard the sea but it was only the sound of a distant highway.

My journey from the Baltic to the Black Sea had been jumbled. The trip had a beginning, middle and end but, thanks to Zita's whims, not in that order. I still had to see the Black Sea. 'Well, if we're going to Romania,' she said, 'we go to Moscow too.'

'We? And who said anything about Moscow?'

'I did. Yesterday or this morning, whenever the bloody hell it was. I've lost all sense of time. I want to go to Moscow.'

'We came to get your teeth now you've got them. You're less than six hundred kilometres from Berlin. Go home.' I felt my aunt had travelled far enough. She was tired and, in any case, I selfishly longed for a full night's sleep, undisturbed by Zita's snores or Winston's farts.

'I don't want to go back to that old dump. There's nothing left for me in Berlin. Let's go to Bucharest.'

'Why on earth do you want to go to Romania?'

'Well, I know someone, don't I.' Zita like an old sailor had a friend in every port.

'Of course.'

'A story-teller. You'll be bloody thankful when you've met him.'

'The car might not make it.'

'*I* might not make it but, what the hell, a girl's got to try.'

We rose to the smell of chicory and the creak of the farmer's leather boots. The house sat in a wooden village. A patchwork of fragmented plots checkered the surrounding slopes. A couple, husband and wife, stood arm in arm beside a small lot, ploughed and newly planted with potatoes.

The Trabant was not well. I cleaned the plugs and adjusted the timing. I poured its petrol-oil mix, which had dripped overnight into carefully placed saucepans, back into the tank. The engine's gaskets were in a frightful state but Zita was determined to go on and, in truth, I didn't want to leave her alone.

Winston was to accompany us, of course. The pig had become vast. Zita could no longer pick him up. His weight had crushed her hat box during the commotion of our arrival in Warsaw. But nothing would persuade her to leave him behind, which made packing the car difficult. In fact, like married couples who grow to look like each other, Winston had come to resemble the car, low-slung and of heavy girth. Zita proposed that we find him a harem of sows – six or eight – to keep him happy in his old age. But until then there was less and less room on the back seat for ourselves. Thankfully, my aunt had seen fit to leave Stalin's nose with Jerzy and Andrzej. They planned to melt it down into souvenir busts of the Pope.

We drove east and south along the edge of the Bieszczady mountains, through bucolic pastures and apricot orchards, past towns of long arcades and pastel shades, once at the edge of Austro-Hungary, now at the end of Poland. The steppe-lands of flaking churches and endless beet fields looked only to the east. It hadn't always been so. Once the cities were filled by Orthodox Jews with ringlets wearing long gabardines, vigorous German merchants and Polish cavalry officers, descendants of Jan Sobieski's Husaria, in smart breeches and riding boots. They lived their lives between East and West, between Christian crusaders and Sarmatian magnates, spoke French and Turkish, built Italianate palaces for their Russian wives. But no more; East and West had been divided.

Poland once shared a border with Romania but since the last war eighty miles of land had separated the two countries. Stalin stole vast tracts of Poland for its oil. Bessarabia and northern Bukovina were annexed from Romania. He peeled away a slice of Hungary. Estonia, Latvia and Lithuania lost their independence so he could access the Baltic. He severed uranium-rich Ruthenia, the eastern tail of Slovakia. The curtain dropped and millions of people, who became Soviet citizens against their will, lost half the world.

Stalin wasn't the first to move borders, simply the most ruthless. Just before dusk we passed near the village of Novoye Selo, called Tiszaújhely in Hungarian. A man called András Orosz lived there. Over the course of his ninety-one years he had held five different nationalities: Austro-Hungarian, Romanian, Czech, Hungarian and, finally, Soviet. Yet Orosz had never once left his village. The borders had been moved around him.

The wheels hummed on the rough asphalt. Our family history unravelled with the miles. The untangled threads led to truths long forgotten and tied Zita to realities which she had never before faced. She sat quietly in the back with Winston, petting his plump flank, staring out on the dying day. My aunt didn't have to travel. She could have stayed at home behind the garden gate. But forgetting no longer helped her cope. She needed to know her place, to rediscover where she stood. Her fantasies had reality and realities segments of fantasy. The truth would issue from both.

Zita shut her eyes and fell asleep, comforted by Winston's presence. He lay his great head on her lap and dreamt. The sun set at our backs and stained the horizon the colour of ashes of roses.

ROMANIA

Man Thinks, God Laughs

NOTHING IN ROMANIA is ever as it seems. No word has true meaning. No action can be judged at face value. We crossed the border at twilight. Tired recruits in dated flannel tunics, Kalashnikovs slung over shoulders, yawned at their posts. Travellers, muffled in their winter coats, whispered, huddled in the pool of light around the window which had swallowed our papers. A curtain hid the inspector's face but his disembodied hands shuffled passports like playing cards. A soldier ran from nowhere to nowhere else, the sharp snap of his strap on gun-metal. Voices were hushed, half heard as in half-sleep. Everyone wished to be in bed but knew they would have no bed that night.

By the side of the road stood a statue, its hand raised as if in blessing. The statue sneezed. It was a hitchhiker, a priest begging a lift. We offered him a ride. He wore a matted mane of black hair and a shaggy beard. Beyond him rose another figure, a soldier, who was hungry. 'Help a starving Romanian,' he said and asked for ten dollars.

We drove through the night along the spine of the Carpathians, across the heel of the horseshoe into the steppe-lands of Moldavia. It had begun to rain heavily and the windscreen wipers packed up. I strung a shoe lace from each back through the side windows. The priest and I drew the wipers by hand back and forth across the glass while Zita tried to sleep. He was going to photograph the painted churches and asked us to join him. I was happy for the guide.

'It is a long drive,' said the priest, his clear brown eyes the colour of worn leather. 'Perhaps you would like if I told you the story of my life. It is a happy story. It will lighten the journey.'

'Tell me.'

'If I do you must promise to tell me a joke. This is the only sadness in being a priest, people forget I am flesh and blood. I like to have a good laugh too.'

His name was Father Dinu, Romanian by birth, Hungarian by blood – a Reformed Church pastor in an Orthodox world, a foreigner in his own land.

His story began at school. In his final year a teacher had asked the class about their plans. The other students answered that they wanted to be engineers on the Danube Canal or drivers of the sleek new Bucharest metro but Dinu confessed, 'I want to teach Latin in South America.' He should have lied. The class laughed. The dream was forbidden.

'How will you get there?' prodded the teacher.

'In a legal way, if possible.'

The teacher, a dwarf too short to see over the lectern, drew himself up to his full height. 'If you were trying to get there illegally,' he warned, 'we would have to tell the police.' The confession cost him both America and a place at university.

Dinu had a choice: to lie or say nothing at all. He chose silence and became a woodcutter in the mountains. For three years he lived alone without desire for human companionship. But one cold Christmas his food ran out. Heavy snow had disrupted supplies. Reluctantly he trudged down the valley to the village. He hadn't eaten for three days or seen a human face in three months. The warm glow of candlelight enticed him to the church. When he opened the heavy door song seemed to fill the whole valley. He joined the Communion and, kneeling at the altar starved of friendship and food, the wine and bread exploded in his mouth like a kiss. He saw for the first time the villagers and was filled with love. He saw himself and was filled with shame. His God-given gift, his life, was being wasted.

'I had thought that there was no one, that I was alone,' he said, 'but I had forgotten that angels walk beside us.'

The woodcutter became a priest. His physical strength mirrored his moral conviction. His sermons drew the faithful from across the valley into his church.

'Face to face,' said Dinu, 'people had forgotten how to be honest. For years they were only able to speak about the mundane – the weather or their shoe size – not what they felt or believed or doubted. Everyone was a spy, everyone was to be distrusted.' As he spoke his shoulders bent forward like a boxer prepared to fight. 'In my church I taught them to speak from their hearts.'

But priests were paid by the state and supervised by a local Party Secretary upon whom they depended for the annual renewal of their state licence to preach. The church hierarchy believed that collusion was the only means of survival. Dinu unsettled the precarious political balance. He was exiled to a drab industrial parish. Yet even there he was too dangerous, his honesty too provocative, and they banished him to an Orthodox village with less than a dozen believers. A police informer was his only regular parishioner. He would attend every sermon and uncross his arms only to take notes or pick his nose.

Life was difficult for the Hungarian minority: their language could not be broadcast or taught and their villages, like others in Romania, were threatened with 'systemization'; their homes were destroyed and the inhabitants resettled in industrial garden cities – concrete deserts without gardens and without industry. Dinu had been in Timişoara during the previous December. There the defiance of another priest, also an ethnic Hungarian, had sparked the revolution. 'The people had had enough. They had no food, no heat. For five days there was street fighting. Tanks fired on the crowd. "Veniţi cu noi," they shouted to the soldiers, "Come with us," but they were shot.' Dinu thrust his hands forward, an advance of tank, leaned his body to the left, a counter strike of demonstrators, as if fighting the battle all over again. 'I saw a boy trampled to death. His mother threw a stone at a tank and the tank ran her down. It was terrible.' Eastern Europe's bloodless revolution had claimed its first victims.

'You promised me a happy story, Father.'

'But it is. Suddenly, like a gift from God, every tank flew the white flag. The army withdrew and the soldiers waved. The loudspeakers blared 'Libertate'. Liberty. The government had fallen. It was a miracle. We had won.' Or so he thought.

'And you?'

'I? I became a man.'

'What do you mean?'

'Well, free.'

Zita mumbled something indecipherable in her sleep.

The showers fell in sheets. Through the night obelisks rose up at us, sodden branches closed in on us. The eyes of animals, caught in our headlights, flashed blood red like demons busy by the roadside. The bleak horizon, strung across barren reaches of stone, tumbled away to nothing at a cliff edge. It was not a hospitable place.

Nor was Succava. By dawn the rain had eased to a dirty drizzle and a filthy mist shrouded the colours of Stefan the Great's capital. Everything was grey. A cripple with a rubber glove for a hand spat in his handkerchief. Men and women with pallid complexions hunched in queues. Methane-fuelled buses, their windows opaque with condensation, rocked workers to factories. Exhaust vapour hung in the air too melancholic to disperse.

Zita blinked at the morning. She had mislaid her teeth in the night but found them in her shoe, the one place in the car where Winston was unlikely to stick his snout.

Dinu directed us along a line of uniform blocks six stories tall. Behind ten thousand doors in dank, damp kitchens, husbands were slumped between table and sink drinking grainy sweet coffee and dropping cigarette ash down plug-holes. Ten thousand wives stood beside them, probably coughing, and refilled their cups from the saucepan on the stove.

A woman in a kerchief pushed a wheelbarrow of wood through the puddles. Loudspeakers blared public announcements about a bakery strike and the evil of Ceauşescu. The dictums, repeated until the words lost all meaning, were as inescapable as the child's wail which pierced the estate. Dinu led us up crumbled concrete stairs toward the cry. He tapped on a door. No response. He knocked harder. Nothing. He hammered with his fist. Elena opened the door. She wore an old woman's face: sunken cheeks, long pointed nose, deep-set eyes. Only her soft skin, pulled so tightly over her skull as to be creaseless, suggested her true age. In her arms was the squalling infant and behind her was her mother.

'Who are you?' demanded the mother, slit eyes in a fat peasant face. Dinu offered her a letter of introduction from a mutual friend. She was suspicious. He introduced us. In the gloom of the hallway the slit eyes rested on me and calculated. She smiled.

Broad hands ushered us into the apartment. 'My guests,' she said. The ravaged building had deceived us, their flat was spacious and carpeted. Elena turned off the video and prepared tea. Pious ikons of, remarkably, laughing saints graced the walls. Mother sat us down, asked questions, inspected our gifts of fruit and wine. Winston, she assumed, was part of the offering and she pinched his haunches before we hastily explained. She never told us her name. 'You have come to see the painted churches? They are very beautiful. Stefan cel Mare was a great king. An honest man.' In the sixteenth century the warrior prince of Moldavia and enemy of the Turks built fourteen churches and monasteries, enclosed by fortified walls, adorned, inside and out, with resplendent frescoes.

Tea appeared. 'Cake, Elena,' ordered Mother. She was a doctor, a general practitioner. 'Do you have a car?' she asked. 'Then you will need a guide. I will find someone.' She shouted to the kitchen, 'Elena. The negresses.' Soft sweet squares concocted from chocolate substitute were produced.

'It's a miracle,' said the doctor as she poured tea. 'Two months ago I could not invite foreigners into the house. If we had spoken on the street I had to report the conversation to the Securitate. Now we can speak as friends. Milk?'

The child, too intrigued to cry, lay on the floor with Winston. She stuck a finger in the pig's eye. Winston squealed and hid behind Zita who had clutched her jaw in pain. The sugar had wormed under her dentures. I picked up the child and offered it cake. 'No,' snapped Elena too sharply. 'She's eaten.' The baby promptly peed on me.

Elena took Lucia and led me to the bathroom. Washing lines stretched overhead. A viewless window stared blindly into a gloomy lightwell. The single cold-water tap dripped into a full tub. Water, like electricity, could be unexpectedly cut off.

Elena gave me a rag and began to change Lucia. She avoided my questions. When she did speak it was without a hint of emotion as if reciting a bus timetable. 'This is my mother's house. She wants you to stay.'

'The three of you live here?'

'Plus my grandmother.' She unpegged a cloth nappy from the line and gestured to a closed door. Four generations of women in a cold-water flat but only her mother worked and doctors were paid less than manual labourers. Their island of luxury in the sea of deprivation left an impression of deceit, like a fine silk suit on a haggard whore.

Dinu had told me that Elena was a writer. I asked if she wrote for one of the many independent newspapers which had sprung up since the revolution.

'For sure I write,' she replied, 'but for a Western magazine. It is possible now. I cannot concern myself with politics. I have a daughter. Could you hold this, please?' She wiped her child's bottom. I asked which magazine.

'I write what you call pornography, the letters column: "My girlfriend can only achieve an orgasm if her Schnauzer, et cetera, et cetera." ' She laughed, unguarded for one moment, and talced her daughter. 'Does it surprise you? I have Lucia to support.'

'And the father?'

'Lucia is *un copil din flori* – a child of the flowers.' Illegitimate. 'Birth control was illegal in Romania.' I felt the embarrassment of sudden intimacy; of strangers who unexpectedly touch or the son at his father's funeral who confesses, 'I never kissed him.'

'Ceauşescu was an evil man,' the doctor explained. 'Life is better now. There is food in the shops and electricity all day. We can use as many light bulbs as we can find, not just two as before.'

Dinu nodded. 'Now I too have hope,' he volunteered. 'Did you see? The soldiers who executed Ceauşescu crossed themselves first. In the end they still have faith.'

'Such is life and so is the world. It's because of Iliescu; he is a man of good faith,' she added.

Elena sat Lucia near Winston. 'After the revolution I felt free inside like never before, but now I feel pity for my dead and buried hopes.'

'My daughter knows nothing.'

'They have killed the dog but kept the chain,' she said and her child again poked Winston's eye.

The lights flickered and went out. 'Terrorists,' said Elena's mother then snapped into Romanian. French is a language of curves, German of parallel lines, Italians converse in spirals and Hungarians at right angles but Romanian is the tongue of ever-decreasing circles.

The women didn't speak to each other but exchanged bursts of fire like machine-gunners at the Somme. Elena's voice became mechanical again. 'Lucia and I can take you to the churches.'

In the dim morning light Zita looked tired. Her lower lip protruded in a scowl, like Churchill piqued. 'I have to recover first,' she grunted. 'I'm not the youngest any more.'

'You must rest,' ingratiated the doctor. 'First you sleep.'

We drove north away from the city's filth into the heart of Moldavia. Sandy paths twisted through emerald fields which rolled toward the Ukraine. A shepherd lazed by his flock. Two hens, their feet bound, dangled from a bicycle's handlebars. Buxom women, cardigans straining over ample bosoms, tilled the earth by hand. Their husbands lashed spindly horses and their children planted potatoes. Leathery old women in kerchiefs drew water from wells headed with gazebos of wood and glass. They gossiped and gesticulated with the crippled gestures of gnarled hands. The dust was stirred by scrawny chickens and fat geese.

The villages were clustered along Roman roads lined by flowering trees with white painted trunks. Every home was fenced with elaborately carved *porţi* or gateways which proclaimed a family's prosperity. The houses were built in stages over a number of years: first of logs, the winter wind howling through the gaps in the rough wood, then a lattice of wooden slats was attached when money allowed. Finally straw and plaster were applied and the surface decorated with intricate floral designs.

A gallery of fir-lined slopes unfolded and Voroneţ, like a brightly illuminated Bible, lay open in a dark green meadow. The church curved as nature about it. No line was straight. The shingled roof was cambered to the roll of the hills. Beneath its great overhanging eaves, the walls were pages of a book, painted in gold and azure. The west wall wove the story of the Last Judgement. God, portrayed in a triptych and held aloft by angels, rose at the apex. Below him stood Christ circled in radiance and surrounded by apostles. A river of fire, the Gehenna, slashed diagonally across the wall and divided Paradise from eternal torment. On one side St Paul led the devout to Judgement, on the other Moses plunged the sinners, all turbaned Turks, down to Hell. The souls of the Christian dead arose as a concourse of Saints entered Paradise.

Nuns with black cylindrical caps, home-knitted sweaters and artless eyes talked us up the thirty steps from Hell to Heaven. Each step represented a mortal sin. Rows of angels aided the faithful ascending the Virtuous Ladder. They speared winged demons who tempted the fallen from the ladder into the mouth of the satanic beast.

Dinu set up his tripod and carefully removed the camera from its bag. He composed his shots with painstaking care. The colours seemed aflame in the afternoon sun but the blue of the church at Voroneţ, a deep cobalt of malachite and iron as livid as plum, and the green of Suceviţa could never be captured or reproduced. The secret of the pigments had been lost.

The churches were built when the country was under siege, cut off from Constantinople. Armies massed behind the fortified gates and waited to do battle with the Turks. The paintings, at once universal and specific, fired the soldiers' patriotism. The Virgin was portrayed as a Byzantine princess and Christ wore a Moldavian shirt. Archangels sounded the Resurrection with *bucium*, wooden Carpathian shepherds' horns. King David played a *cobza*, a Romanian lute. In depicting the seventh-century defence of Constantinople the Persians were dressed as Turks, the courageous defenders as Moldavians.

Elena breathed deeply and relaxed away from her mother. 'It's a wonderful fresh air,' she said. 'I like being far away from the civilized world.'

The engine stalled on the road to Putna. The car seemed to have lost its spark with the burial of Mirek. It was as if his soul had spirited us forward, but now the Trabant gave up the ghost and we coasted to a stop.

'Oh, fantastic,' said Zita.

Dinu and I looked under the bonnet. Zita shook her head. 'The little beastie and I are going for a walk.' As they rummaged over the carpet of marsh marigolds I heard her ask, 'Where the ruddy hell are we, Winston?'

I was no mechanic. My usual method was to hit every exposed part with a screwdriver handle, tighten the odd nut and hope. But I thought the problem might be electrical and wrapped the fuses in silver cigarette paper. Zita would be displeased, her duty-frees now loose in a carrier bag, especially as the car still didn't start. I turned the key and the Trabant wheezed an asthmatic gasp.

'You disapprove of me because I am a pornographer?' Elena had slipped out of the car and her shoes without a sound. She stood barefoot in the dust, Lucia perched on her hip. 'That is all right, it is more comfortable to put labels on things. But this is just a part of the truth, which is worse than a lie.'

It was difficult to imagine her at home, as she washed nappies and stewed carrots, inventing provocative sexual problems. I wondered if Grandmother helped? I imagined sex in Succava could only be bereft of eroticism. It provided comfort, certainly, but probably precious little other joy.

'I have to live my life on a realistic basis. All I want is to buy some things for Lucia, not much, a little house – with a kitchen and a bathroom – and a place where she can have a hammock and sleep like a fish in a fishing net.' Her English was lucid, learnt from books but rarely before spoken. Many words she had translated directly from Romanian, assuming similar Latin roots conveyed identical modern meanings. Elena looked askance, out of the corner of brown eyes, her whole head tilted back as if in suspicion.

'You know it is not like my mother says. We have to make real investigations to get what we need, sometimes at the back door, giving tips and acting friendly with the shop man. And the shops are almost empty now that we have "democracy". We have to be content with very few food and no medicine, even those of great need for stomach and heart. We are walking on moving sand.'

'But your table is full,' said Dinu. 'You should be thankful for God's gifts.'

'They are from my mother's garden. She is a person of low quality.' The pornographer judged the doctor.

A horse and cart passed us. Tassels hung from the mare's bridle and red wool was entwined in her tail and mane. Three men rode in the back. Each wore a fleece hat and a dark, dishevelled suit, each held a child dressed in home-knitted trousers and a woollen bobble hat. They didn't stop.

The priest spread a picnic – kindly prepared by Elena's mother – on the roof of the car while I siphoned off the petrol. The distributor cap had been damp and I suspected that there was water in the tank. Elena ate little and fed Lucia only on packaged food. It was no wonder the child looked pale. A band of Gypsies, young and defiant, appeared on the road. They walked as one, clasped together as a single beast, a hydra of reeling heads and tentacles. The car was surrounded. The boys mocked the engine. The girls feigned disinterest and demanded gum. Suddenly the leader, a stocky bully with a provocation of bristle, slapped his girl. His honour, somehow, had been slighted and he spat accusations. She laughed it off. The group gripped, grasped and danced a mating rite as power shifted. Her allies withdrew and the girl was isolated, her supplications ignored. The boys closed the circle to cut her out then turned their backs. The hydra lost a head.

The beast vanished as quickly as it had appeared when the police arrived. The Romanies had been tortured or murdered under the old regime. Officially the persecution had stopped with the revolution but as suspicions lingered the band didn't. Dinu instinctively put away his Praktika.

In the back of the police car sat Zita, looking excited, with Winston by her side. 'Did you hear it? The cuckoo? I heard the first cuckoo of spring.' The door didn't open from the inside. 'For heaven's sake, let me out,' she ordered. The police didn't share her enthusiasm for fauna. They puffed with self-importance.

'They're completely around the twist,' said Zita as she clambered free. 'They started waving their blasted guns about and everything. Poor Winston nearly had a fit.' She had been found on the road without papers but with a pig. They had assumed she had stolen it.

'Absolutely ridiculous I told them. Where could I steal one? These two', she said pointing at her captors, 'are the only swine left in Romania.' Before the revolution every pig was exported to earn hard currency, only the trotters could remain in the country. A pair had been hung on Ceauşescu's grave after his assassination.

I gave the police Zita's passport.

'Go on,' she said and shook their hands. 'I accept your apology. If you can't make mistakes, what can you do?' Thankfully, Zita didn't speak Romanian. Elena explained and they seemed satisfied.

'Isn't this ruddy tin can running yet?' enquired my aunt. 'How about a push and bump? The boys will help.'

Somehow she persuaded them. Elena refused to get involved. She told us that recently the police had been subjected to an intelligence test. Every officer was given a board punched with various shaped holes and the corresponding pegs. They were asked to insert the right peg into the right hole. The results were encouraging. It was found that two per cent of policemen were very intelligent and ninety-eight per cent were very, very strong. The flatfoots who push-started the car were among the majority. The Trabant had never moved so fast.

'Just don't say anything,' instructed Zita when we were back on our way. 'At least the cuckoo's song was very beautiful.'

'It must be frustrating being a policeman,' mused Dinu. 'We used to fear them but now they are told to work within the law.'

'I wonder', asked Elena, 'if law and freedom can ever co-exist?'

'Not that old chestnut,' moaned my aunt.

Law for Dinu and Elena was not of the people, for the people. It was the dictate of an élite imposed by force on the oppressed. Law had meant injustice.

'For sure it is the same as the church,' said Elena. 'We learnt at school that Christianity is an instrument used to exploit people.

Like the law.' She laughed. 'You can imagine what sort of history we were taught.'

'My child,' said Dinu, his fingers splayed as if to catch the ether of her soul, 'God is love.'

'I'm not your child.' She held her daughter in her arms. 'She is all I love and I am my own god.'

The spirit of society had been fractured. Laws did not reflect the will of the people. God was not a righteous judge, strong and patient, but an instrument of repression. The young didn't know Him.

'It's different for you, you can have a pleasant life – useful and clean.' Elena smiled her crooked smile, wily but not to be distrusted. 'You mock my ignorance but I am a child of communism. I have been corrupted by it.' We rode in silence to Putna, the last of the churches.

It was sunset and the chants of the monks merged with the wind in the pines. Putna's defensive walls, bereft of frescoes, stood stark white against the forest. In contrast, its interior seemed shrouded in funereal crêpe. The air was thick with incense and the light dimmed by vapours. Candles hissed and spat, blackening the pillars. Centuries of soot and damp had corroded the paint. Smoke rose into the inky dome where Christ, with great raven eyes, glared from a universe of stars. The monks were unseen and their eerie voices muffled. The mass was celebrated behind the iconostasis, the sacred screen which stretched across the width of the church, a curtain between altar and nave. Here heaven and earth were divided. Here Occident and Orient were parted, not by Turks, but by an idea.

Christendom's fault-line between Rome and Constantinople was not an historical curiosity but a division of worlds. In the west the Protestants, the protesters, had torn down the screens. Their ideas came to be accepted in most of the Catholic world. The Renaissance, the Reformation and the Enlightenment, the interconnected upheavals which created the modern world, championed individual consciousness. Every individual became answerable directly to God. But the upheavals took place outside Orthodoxy. In the east the church, through its priests, remained an intermediary: middlemen between man and the Almighty.

Individuals were answerable to the priest, who slipped behind the iconostasis and sorted out their destiny with God. It was a dictatorship of faith. The priest alone heard the word of God. The law was based on doctrine not debate. The society accepted that a mortal, flawed as all men, could administer divine power.

Bells tolled, the Royal doors opened and the priest emerged. He chanted in ancient liturgical Slavonic, words unchanged for a thousand years. A ray of evening sunlight caught the gold thread of his Easter surplice. He held the chalice, the bread and wine, to administer the Sacrament.

'Pretty,' whispered Elena. 'But what's the point?'

I found Dinu outside. He sat beside a lilac bush, framed by clusters of deep violet flowers. His calloused hands hung limply by his sides.

'I had begun to think', he said, 'that the priority was making the economy work. It's not. It is the spirit of the people which must be rebuilt.'

Roses were placed in the centre of the table. The rich blooms, grown under glass in the allotment, were tightly closed. The stretched fleece of a lamb dried on the balcony. Its flesh, minced and spiced with wild thyme, made the meatloaf for dinner. Dinu said grace. Elena's mother raised a glass of *ţuica*, crisp plum brandy. 'Eat, my friends, and see how well we eat. *Poftă bună, bon appétit.*' She and Elena knocked coloured Easter eggs together until they cracked. 'Christ has risen,' the godless chanted, 'truly he has risen.'

'In Romania we eat one and a half times more than you and,' the doctor nodded at the dentures wrapped in a tissue on the table, 'our dentists are better too.'

Zita explained about her teeth. For years a mysterious ailment had poisoned her system. It could not be diagnosed. By chance an infected tooth had to be removed. Her dentist was appalled by the decay it revealed. When all the remaining teeth were pulled out her health improved.

'Marigolds,' prescribed the doctor. 'Soaked overnight in water, warmed and drunk in the morning. Every day. That would have saved them.'

'What the blazes. They're dead and gone now.'

'It cures cancer too.' Her home remedies claimed to have saved
the life of a friend. 'Priests must be careful with their throats,'
she advised Dinu. 'Linden leaves are best for bronchitis, camomile for digestion.' She had grown up on the land. Her father,
a labourer on a plum orchard, taught her nature's secrets. She
had little respect for medical science and only became a doctor
because the education board needed to fulfil a five year plan.

'And blueberries,' she added. 'All my aunts and uncles went
blind. It's in our blood.' She gestured at a closed door. 'I've fed
my own mother blueberries for forty years and she has eyes like
a bat.'

The allotment was the doctor's passion: there she kept chickens
and a turkey, grew herbs and great heads of cauliflower. Away
from the stink of Suceava and the unheated hospital with three
patients to a bed, she would bury her hands in the earth and feel
whole.

The food was the best we ate in Romania. Zita mumbled a
compliment as she sucked on an enormous gherkin. 'No wedding without bread, no funeral without laughter. I do it all
myself,' bragged the doctor. 'My daughter never helps me. She's
too busy with that child.' Elena, who had eaten little, went into
the bedroom and returned with Lucia. The child had woken from
a nightmare and her face was bleach white.

The doctor wanted to know about the West: the price of a loaf
of bread and a house in Hampstead. When I answered she hissed,
a remarkable sound like an enraged swan.

'You'll need some lei for your stay in our country,' she said
suddenly. 'It's dangerous to change money on the street. You'll
be cheated. I'd be happy to arrange it for you.'

We did need currency but had changed some illegally with
Elena that morning. She was saving to buy a house and had
asked us to keep our arrangement quiet. Lei and lies. I apologized
to the doctor explaining that we had changed money elsewhere.
Her face set into an expressionless mask.

'He was a tall man,' said Zita in an attempt to give the lie
substance, 'with a small head and very big glasses.'

'It's not easy for us, you know.' The doctor eyed Elena.

'The true riches are in heaven,' suggested Dinu. 'But it's nice to have a little pocket money before we get there.'

'I work at the hospital all day, evenings and Sunday on the land while she,' the doctor pointed accusingly, 'she just sits.'

Elena refused to rise to the bait. 'I know that I cannot afford to remain a child as long as I have a child myself.' She held her daughter. 'And a very sweet one too. So I write my articles,' she concluded softly, then slapped Lucia's hand as she reached for a slice of apple. The child wailed. It seemed hungry.

'You should be ashamed of that smut. What does it pay for? Certainly not the child. We didn't need another mouth to feed.'

'All my friends had abortions,' Elena said plainly. 'Their wombs are ruined.'

The government had wanted to increase the country's population. Abortions were forbidden for women with less than five children. 'Demographic command units' examined females at their work-place every three months. Pregnancies had to be registered. Fertility control became a criminal offence. It was not uncommon for a woman, between the ages of twenty and thirty, to have seven or eight abortions. A quarter of Romania's women had been mutilated.

'Stupid girls,' clicked the doctor. 'They went to amateurs, nursing assistants or orderlies. They should have gone to a professional.'

Elena held her child. 'With what? Doctors charged a month's salary. A month's.'

'You didn't have to worry about money.'

'I wanted someone to love. She's all I have.'

As we spoke the heat from the overhead light warmed the roses. Their petals spread, heavy and wet. From under the leaves and within the buds crawled minute lacquer-black beetles. They dried their wings and flew, swarming over the dinner table, into our food, our wine, our hair. They seized their few brief moments of life and mated on the rose petals.

'I do not know how you can eat this food grown on that land.' Elena was standing, shaking as she spoke, 'All those dead babies – it is horrible.'

By Saturday the bread strike had been settled. In the run-up to the election the 'interim' government, the National Salvation Front, bought peace. Party funds were spent to win favour and the disputes didn't last. Demands were met. There was food in the shops for a few weeks.

It was a relief to eat the bread. It was grey, the colour of cement, with pockets of uncooked dough under the crust, but its wheat had been fertilized by orthodox methods. A customer in the queue raved to us, 'It's a miracle. Now we can buy bread *and* cheese *and* sausage.' Before the revolution Romanians often survived on bread alone. It gave us a stomach ache, of course, and the doctor produced beakers of camomile tea to settle the ferment.

The Romanians were not a courageous people. They had always survived as best they could by cheating and lying. They deserved better but failed, with few exceptions, to demand more. Why? Ceauşescu had been a dictator but how much had individual Romanians defied him? They needed gods to deify and consume. Authority was feared but discipline loved. On a tram I had overheard a passenger say, 'If Ceauşescu had given me more to eat, I'd have kissed his ass.' The people had been degraded so that they might be squashed underfoot like silver-fish on a urinal floor.

We said our goodbyes. Father Dinu asked if we would drive him to Sighişoara. He felt uneasy in Moldavia. 'And you haven't told me that joke,' he reminded me. Zita and I collected our bags but the doctor, thick arms crossed, blocked the doorway. Her attitude towards us had altered after we had refused to exchange money.

'You've eaten my food, drunk my wine, slept in my beds. A hotel would charge you $100 for the night. Let's call it fifty. Each.' After we'd paid she warned, 'Watch out for the terrorists.'

Riding with the Best Man

'SHE IS LONG SKIRT and short mind,' said Kristan pointing across the gully between tower blocks at a woman dressing by her window. She twisted left and right before the mirror, smoothed the material to her hips and cocked her head. 'She knows I am watching and she is doing it for me.' How she knew puzzled me as our curtains were drawn. 'I will have her. No problem.'

Father Dinu had led us to Sighişoara, a confined, medieval Transylvanian town of ochre and lavender. Kristan's parents, old friends of the priest, had welcomed us like long lost relatives. In a way we were; their family were Saxons and had lived in the Carpathians for thirty generations. Before the December revolution the ethnic Germans numbered a quarter of a million, but in the few months since the borders were opened they had fled, abandoning home and history, back to the Fatherland they had never seen. A community, established in Romania almost as long as the Normans in Britain, had disintegrated. Kristan's family planned to join the exodus within the month.

A tenuity of cloth, lace in our imaginations, cupped her breasts. Her skin was tawny, a rich red like baked clay. She could have been either Gypsy or Slav.

'Not Gypsy,' said Kristan. 'They live over there in the Congo. They make love like wolves and tear your skin until you bleed. Slavs lie back and think of the harvest. She's a Slav and I want to pick her like a ripe plum and pop her in my mouth.'

Zita snoozed in the next room, a nap which would give her fleas. She'd pass them to me and I'd give them to Winston; sharing was important in our family. When the woman had finished dressing and left her window, Kristan took me to the

Congo. On the stairs he paused to argue with two neighbours about a light bulb. It had burnt out and accusations were made as to who used it most. Kristan singled out the shift worker who worked nights. He used the hall light most so he must pay. 'I will sell you the bulb at a reduced rate,' he offered. Kristan was a business man.

The Congo was a rotten Habsburg barracks. Gypsies had requisitioned the ruins and naked children played in the mud while their parents slumped in stoops. Open fires burnt at the centre of smoke-filled billets. Kristan's passage was ignored. 'The Gypsies have the best sources of supply. But there are places they cannot go,' he told me. 'They would be murdered. So, no problem, I fill a niche in the market. I will do well in the West, yes?'

Only through the black market could any kind of normal life be preserved. The planned economy had overlooked many daily necessities. Kristan bartered for light bulbs with American cigarettes and sold razor blades for dollars. On the walk back to his block he seemed pleased.

'Look here.' He held up a single pack of Kent, Romania's second currency. On the black market it would cost the equivalent of two days' salary. 'Do you see the seam?' The cellophane sleeve seemed intact. 'I cut it here,' he pointed, 'and replace American cigarettes with Romanian. It increases my profit margin.' He was proud of his ruse.

'But what happens when you're found out?'

He brushed the thought aside. 'No one smokes them for months. They are traded back and forth a dozen times. And by the time they are traced back to the Congo I will be long gone.' He paused at the entrance and nodded at her estate opposite. It was white and new and nicknamed the Vatican. Every building had a pseudonym. Kristan's block, the oldest in a long stretch of tenements, was a wasteland called the Bărăgan after the desolate and wind-swept Muntenian plain.

'I cannot sleep for thinking of her,' he confessed. 'I have to get up in the night and look out. She is always there turning this way or that.' He looked at his watch and sighed, 'She is the only thing I will miss when we leave this prison.'

The medieval heart of Sighişoara was daubed with plum, lilac and burgundy colours. Its roofs were russet tiled and its lanes bronze cobble-stoned. Once I had imagined eastern Europe in shades of black and white, as a ghetto of monochromatic deprivation. The misconception needed to be tinted in unfamiliar colours: the ochre of Prague's Hradčany, the blue of Voroneţ, the lavender of Sighişoara.

Winston climbed the sloping streets under the tight cluster of gables and eaves. Slender towers rose at each crook of the steep city walls. The Bergkirche, from where feudal knights might have rescued captive damsels, crowned the hill.

Transylvania was a citadel within the arc of the Carpathians. Roman legions had driven into the dark woods to mine its gold. Magyars ruled the plateau for one thousand years and settled the Saxons in its towns to defend the marches of their empire. The Germans transformed the wattle and daub hamlets into important trading centres. They erected noble buildings and created settlements of beauty where before there had been nothing. Sighişoara was one of their seven fortified towns, built in the twelfth century to withstand the ravages of Turks and Tartars. But the mountain walls, which had long protected the settlers, became a prison, trapping people in ghettos of intolerance. Transylvania was torn between Hungary and Romania like a child denied Solomon's judgement. Suspicions bred, neighbour turned against neighbour, grudges were borne like banners and men defined their identity by hatred.

The pig dawdled outside Vlad Dracul, the house of the devil, where bleary voices slurred their words. 'The best beer in Romania is brewed in this valley,' announced Kristan waving his arm over distant beech woods. Then he added quietly, 'but it is not as good as German beer.'

'Winston hasn't drunk Romanian beer and I'm thirsty enough to swill a barrel', exaggerated Zita while she scratched.

Kristan went inside but returned hounded by rabid laughter. 'They will not let a pig inside,' he advised.

'I don't care for their bloody company either. We'll ruddy well drink right here in the street.'

Winston lapped the cloudy liquid from a saucer and burped.

He had developed a taste for beer in Tokaj. Rabelaisian drinkers stared from the pub window. The house, Kristan told us, was the birthplace of Vlad Dracul. Romanians liked to believe that *drac*, the word for devil, was derived from the Dacs, the name of their fiendish ancestors. But the Dracula legend which originated in the mountains was woven out of the infamy of Vlad Dracul's son, Vlad Ţepeş who eliminated his enemies by impaling them with a stake up the rectum. Once he skewered an entire Ottoman delegation in this manner. The root of the name Ţepeş was ţeapa, the Romanian for thorn. Garlic proved a poor defence.

We wove our way up the cobbles to a terraced cemetery. On the top tier the gravestones were engraved in Gothic script and marked the final resting place of the Germans. The middle level was reserved for Hungarians and on the lowest step lay the Romanians.

'Now it has been reversed,' sighed Kristan. 'Ceauşescu once said that there will be no more national minorities in Romania – only one socialist nation. He understood nothing.' Nearby a family ate a picnic of bread, feta and radishes. The children made garlands of dandelions. Their father produced the special treat, an orange, and teased his daughter, rolling it against her cheek before peeling off the skin. But rather than divide the fruit into segments, he bit it like an apple. Their faces streamed with juice. After the years of deprivation the Romanians had forgotten how to eat oranges.

'Oh my God,' wheezed Zita, 'where's Winston?'

We retraced our steps and asked at the pub. The drinkers jeered. No one in the queue outside the bakery had seen him and the police weren't interested. We circled the citadel and, just in case, returned to the cemetery but he was nowhere to be found. Zita lay down by a grave and moaned, 'I'm infested with fleas and Winston's gone. Leave me here to die.'

We didn't, of course. We took her back to the wind-swept plain and consoled her with synthetic banana juice laced with sugar-beet rum. There was nothing else in the flat other than cigarettes and light bulbs so Zita smoked a Kent. I didn't know why she had saddled herself with the inconvenience of the pig. I simply accepted his presence like a pet dog or favourite hat.

But, with his disappearance, I worried about Winston for the first time.

Kristan had business to do in the next town and rather than leave Zita alone we persuaded her to join us. But the Trabant was out of petrol and none would be available until the next morning.

'That is all right,' said Kristan, 'we'll ride with the best man.'

We didn't buy tickets. The train arrived and Kristan directed us into a first-class compartment. He put his merchandise on the luggage rack. Zita hadn't travelled by train for twenty years but the gentle rock of the carriage seemed to comfort her.

'The price is set', explained Kristan as he passed us tickets punched with more holes than a colander, 'at thirty percent of the normal fare.' He folded a banknote under the used ticket. 'Give this to the best man when he comes along. He will keep the cash and punch the ticket. No problem.'

At Romanian weddings guests bring money rather than gifts. The best man is responsible for its collection. Ticket collectors acquired the same title because of their willingness to accept bribes.

'No one pays full price,' Kristan laughed, 'except foreigners, but they are cows to be milked.'

'Then why bother hiding the money?' asked Zita waving the note. Kristan restrained her.

'So no one sees. The fool is not fool enough if he's not proud.'

In Romania corruption was not a vice, it was a tradition. The Greeks of Constantinople, the Phanariots, were a particularly duplicitous people who governed the country when it was an Ottoman vassal. Their voracious greed had perverted the society. The kings and dictators who followed continued to debase public morals. The custom persisted even after the December revolution. In Romania's first free election a million more votes were cast than voters registered. The official news agency attributed the discrepancy to the 'enthusiasm of the people for democracy'.

'Do not misunderstand me,' cautioned Kristan. 'We have principles.' He took pride in the ingenuity and initiative of deception. 'No engineer would ever sell potatoes at the market.'

'But you're an engineer.'

'Exactly, that is why I am selling light bulbs and cigarettes. No problem.' Without a word the conductor punched our tickets and pocketed the bribe. To a Romanian the new democracy meant the freedom to make money.

The sky darkened at midday. The leaden air fell in palls of soot. The earth turned black. Tree trunks were charred like burnt cork. A dirty cloud covered everything in ash. Kristan nodded to our destination, 'Copşa Mică.'

The grime on the station platform penetrated our clothes. Kristan, immediately recognized, was besieged and did business in a corner of a buffet. An old zinc worker in a blackened blue beret proffered tissues of lei with hands the colour of graphite. His eyes were bloody knife slashes, the lower lids wrenched open by the heat, and his mouth was a scar between sunken cheeks. He could barely whisper, his voice box was singed; he wanted razor blades though his hair follicles had been burnt away. A woman without money needed cigarettes to bribe her doctor and offered a chicken. The deal excited Kristan. His eyes glazed over, a look which I had only seen in the West, and seemed quite dead. Zita asked me for tea with lemon, and Winston. I found only ersatz coffee. Soot dusted its surface before the liquid cooled.

Across the rails a dark satanic mill belched pitchy smoke. The Carbocin plant produced *negru de fum*, carbon black, the residue of incinerated oil and gas used in the production of car tyres. Beyond the plant lurked another demon, the IMN factory, which smelted lead and zinc. Endless conveyor belts scraped and squealed beyond the curtains of smoke and somewhere a car horn blared again and again. Slaves, barely human, breathed and moved and toiled within the machine's dark walls. 'They are trapped, of course,' said Kristan as we left the station. 'But after the revolution we realized that we are all among walls like a prison. But you and I, we are different, we can escape.'

A sad town clung to the perimeter of the works. The morning's growth of grass provided the only colour. The luminous shoots of green were smothered by soot within hours. The washing on the line was black. The church steeple was black. The car with the strident horn – a Dacia – and a trailer in tow coughed toxic fumes and circled the streets without apparent purpose.

A peasant, her house not fifty yards from the furnaces, gestured to us. Her garden of inky soil bore flowers in neat rows. She presented Zita with a tulip smudged with tears of black. 'Come back in the autumn,' she suggested, 'and I'll give you the bulb.' Her voice was slow and precise. The Transylvanian accent had been influenced by German. Dogs in the north, it was said, growled 'rrrow-rrrow' while in the Latinate south they barked 'wow-wow'.

In an asphalt beer garden where Kristan sold his last light bulbs, the drinkers regarded us with open hostility but numbed their anger in chipped steins. A labourer counted his pay and passed the bills to Kristan. The black market was an evil necessity. The revolution, full of promise, had changed nothing. The same bureaucrats sat at the same desks, their Party pins replaced by 'Free Romania' arm bands.

A drunkard cried foul. He had spotted the counterfeit Kent. Kristan, after passionate denial, returned his money but the men were riled and levelled well-founded accusations. A glass shattered. The publican picked up the telephone. Kristan collected his bag and walked away.

'Come on,' he ordered. 'They know you are foreigners, you walk without fear.' The years of lies had reinforced the suspicion toward outsiders.

'And you?' I asked as we turned.

'Go on. Get out, kraut,' shouted a drunk, 'and take the Hungarians and Gypsies with you.'

'I am gone,' said Kristan. So was Zita. 'Where is your aunt?'

She was across the road talking to the driver of the Dacia. I took her arm.

'Hold your horses, I can't understand what the blazes this man is saying.'

'Pigs,' said Kristan without thinking and looked over his shoulder at the advancing drunks. 'He is selling pigs.' The farmer, a tall gaunt man with eyebrows which hung like vines, slid out from behind the wheel. He opened the trailer's hatch. Among the hairy Mangalitzas and sleek Edelschwein was a single, smiling Tamworth – Winston.

'Hey, Winston,' shrieked Zita. 'What the blazes is the bastard doing in here?'

'We had better go,' advised Kristan. The men, assembled at the opposite side of the road, shouted abuse. A drunk threw the contents of his glass.

'We can't leave him in here,' said Zita. But Winston seemed content to stay. He'd made a friend. 'He suffers from claustrophobia.' The farmer misunderstood. Zita, he assumed, wanted to negotiate. He knocked off ten per cent. 'You stole him.' He halved the price. 'I wouldn't give you a bloody penny.'

Kristan, his trousers soaked in beer, insisted, 'We must go.'

'I've been worried sick about you,' Zita told her pig.

It all happened at once. Zita reached into the hatch and pulled Winston away from the sow. The drunk took Kristan by the scruff of the neck. Drinkers surrounded the car. The pigs squealed. The farmer, unfamiliar with Zita's negotiation technique, grabbed at Winston. She punched him in the nose. Her back went. The police arrived.

They pushed into the crowd, one tall with a pencil moustache, the other corpulent and sweating. Their uniforms were filthy and their cuffs mustard-stained. They saw us, the dropped cigarettes, the farmer's bloody nose and concluded, 'Terrorists.'

'Tourists,' I corrected.

'Terrorists. Terrorists,' they insisted and slapped the drunk across the face.

'I'll terrorize this bloody thief unless you arrest him,' added Zita unhelpfully.

Our passports didn't interest them. We were hustled into their car. Zita clung to Winston. Kristan guarded his cartons. The drunks were dispersed. The Dacia and its trailer followed us to the police station.

The rain left streaks of soot on the walls. We were confined in a urine-yellow room which smelt of damp. The paint flaked onto the cracked tile floor. A frame, which had once held a portrait of the 'dictator of sad memory', hung empty awaiting a new idol.

The inspector, a sheepish man, never lifted his eyes. Zita clasped Winston to her breast and confessed, 'I socked him in the conk.' The farmer demanded compensation. 'I'm not giving him the day of the week,' she added for good measure.

He clicked his tongue and studied his fingernails. 'In Copşa Mică we have democracy. You disturb.'

'This swine swiped my pig.'

'So you sayed.' The inspector spoke a sort of English. 'Yes. But poof? Poof? Where it is?'

The onus of proof rested on us but Winston's papers had been left in Sighişoara. Tourists rarely travelled with farm animals and farmers generally kept pigs. The inspector shrugged, his conclusion was inevitable. 'Then is farmer's. The low is the low.'

'Put me in your bloody prison,' submitted Zita, 'but you'll not take Winston away.'

The inspector sucked on his teeth. 'No, I think no prison. Has been. Very bad. Bad. You go now.'

Kristan stood. 'Sit, thank you,' said the policeman. He didn't. 'Is it not possible?' he asked and placed his bag, full of cigarettes, on the desk. The farmer leapt to his feet and shouted. The inspector didn't move. Kristan bade us follow. We walked away.

In the train back to Sighişoara I reimbursed Kristan for the cigarettes. 'No problem,' he said.

Zita held Winston. 'Try that trick again and I'll chop your balls off. I'm an old lady. I can do what I want.'

Kristan looked at his watch. 'I will see her tonight.'

'Your girlfriend?'

'No. She is in Bucharest with her belly on her mouth.' She was pregnant. 'But abortion is legal now. No problem. Before it was very expensive.' He laughed. 'Nothing in life is free.'

'Then you mean the Slav?'

He shrugged. 'Of course. Anyway my girlfriend is Romanian and I am not staying. I am going home.' He didn't mean the wasteland. He meant the Germany that he had never seen; the *Drängen nach Westen*. 'It has been going downhill here since the Middle Ages.'

The restaurant was closed and we hadn't eaten all day. In our hotel room Zita and I fell on a cold picnic supper. Without a word we stuffed our mouths with sausage and cheese. We had bought white bread, only available on the black market, and drank a bottle of rough brandy. We were ravenous, but greater than our hunger was the sensation of denigration.

Winston looked at us askance. We had become strangers. He slipped under the bed and watched the beasts argue over the last piece of cheese.

Words Words Words

IT WAS ON A TRAIN that Zita had met Stefan the story-teller. Tucked into the corner of their compartment, travellers gathered like moths around his pool of light, he had cast spells. He had a gift and his stories gave the magic. Stefan spun yarns of struggle and heroism, which drew heavily on rich epic tradition, and reduced life's ambiguities to tales of easy certainty. The children of peasant Europe believed the stories that they were told and their long rail journeys vanished into the night.

Trains moved Stefan. He had been born on the Orient Express. His mother rushed from Paris back to Romania to bear her only child. She went into labour at the border. The conductor, a sweaty surly Slav, assumed the role of mid-wife. A squad of soldiers carried bowls of water, spilling and sloshing, from the locomotive. As he grew older his father, a booking clerk for the railway, took him to watch the trains. Stefan would record in his fine-lined notebook the times of the Sophia or Karpaty Express and the number of wagons on sinuous freights. In the evening before bed he would entertain his mother with invented stories of their passengers and cargo. Trains were his life. He first saw his wife from a train. He met Peter and Zita on a train. He killed a man on a train.

After the war when idealism infected Europe like a fever, Peter was seconded from Hungary to Romania to assist the FND – the National Democratic Front – seize power. Romania's tradition of vote-rigging had been inherited from the last century. Electors were harassed by police, opposition leaders imprisoned and victory assured. Few had the courage to challenge the custom. Stefan was a young activist assigned to help my uncle co-ordinate the recruitment of sympathetic workers. It was the usual pattern:

railway men were issued with metal coshes and sent to the cities to disrupt the November elections. The action was effective.

Together my uncle and the story-teller rode the trains up and down the country. Stefan told tales constantly, his eyes gleaming behind misshapen wire spectacles and scratching his lawless curls of red hair. The power of words both to entertain and mould opinion excited him. In the dark days his stories gave people hope and he came to believe that he could help people see the truth.

On one recruitment trip Stefan alone rode the Transylvania overnight to Cluj. In his compartment travelled a student who had lived part of his short life in France. The young men traded tales, wine and enthusiasm. In eloquent French the student sang the praises of Paris, of the beauty of its women and the majesty of the Seine. Stefan, who had never thought of France, became enthralled. He hung on every word and created Paris in his mind. The stranger wove a web which would snare Stefan for the rest of his days.

The drink loosened their tongues and talk turned to politics. Stefan was certain his new camerade would share his views but instead the stranger revealed himself to be a passionate royalist. He confessed to have returned to Romania to fight for the National Peasant Party – their leaders had already been arrested – and believed passionately in the restoration of the monarchy.

Stefan was appalled. He fell quiet and feigned sleep. But his mind raced through the night. At dawn he could not meet the stranger's eye. He had reached his decision. At Cluj he went to the police and the student was arrested. Later, as the report of the People's Court stated, he hanged himself in custody.

Stefan's vigilance won him great kudos. The privileged world of the *nomenklatura* opened to him. He joined the ranks of the élite who ran the new republic. But he never recovered from the incident and guilt ate away at his conscience like a maggot. He developed severe motion sickness, could no longer travel by train and his days as an agitator ended. He preferred to stay at home sleeping in his familiar bed and eating his familiar meals.

But a story-teller without anyone to tell stories to is an unhappy person. Stefan was offered a position at the Section for

Press and Propaganda. His love of words would make him a writer. But he closed the shutters on the world. Language ceased to be the window of the mind and became instead a curtain to draw across it. Ironically, he was assigned to the French section. His brief was not to inform but to influence. He was to erode Romanian francophilia. His subtle articles changed opinions more than a thousand venomous speeches. Bucharest was no longer the Paris of the Balkans – nor did it want to be.

Stefan possessed the unusual combination of ability and political loyalty. He rose quickly in seniority, moulding words and meanings like putty, but the higher the promotion gained the greater became his remorse. He pushed the official line harder and harder to convince himself that his action had been correct.

France came to obsess him. He would denounce de Gaulle or criticize the decadence of the *seizième arrondissement* then secretly pore over maps of Paris. Both he and his wife taught themselves French. He read compulsively and in his mind's eye girls in flowered bonnets laughed by the Seine. He danced with them until dawn at the Élysée-Montmartre then drank bitter coffee at Les Deux Magots. Yellow sunlight gleamed off copper roofs and painters yawned under umbrellas in La Place du Tertre. He came to know the unknown city better than his own, better, perhaps, than a Parisian.

The wordsmith won favour. He named the despised leader 'the most loved son of the people'. His savage wife became 'the legendary mother of the fairytales of our childhood'. Their dictatorship, with electricity rationed to two hours per day, was coined 'the years of light'. Language lied. Stefan's glib and oily art made writing unreadable. His rhetoric prevented change. Like the secret police with their truncheons and prison cells, it crippled the opposition's ability to express alternative political ideas. His ideologically derived jargon became the only language for debate. He dishonoured words.

Bucharest had been a tinselly, tiny Paris of open spaces and boulevards, of intimate cafés and secluded lakes. Its gentle Latin air once whiffed of the Orient and fluttered with parakeets. At dusk beneath a canopy of limes and chestnuts, couples would promenade along the Calea Victoriei from restaurant to bazaar, to eat with friends or dance at the Athenaeum. But the city's heart had been ripped out. Instead of horse-drawn *trăsuri*, rusty trams rattled along deserted streets. Within the space of a year the genial leader had demolished a dozen churches, two monasteries, a synagogue and nine thousand homes to build his Avenue of the Victory of Socialism. It was as if a road as wide as Park Lane had been thrust from Hyde Park to the Aldwych – gutting Mayfair and Soho *en route*. He modified the town plan with as much judgement as a child playing sand-castles.

In a leafy corner of the second sector the streets were named after composers. Stefan and his wife, Antonietta, lived on Saint-Saens in a small villa embraced by vines and wisteria. A tin Eiffel Tower stood in pride of place on the mantel. Framed Parisian postcards hung on the wall. Antonietta, a hunchback, wore black. She was alone but for a goldfish bowl clasped to her breast.

'Je regrette,' she told us simply, 'mon mari est parti.'

As Romania, stretched on a rack of hateful madness, had slipped toward revolution, the propaganda machine devoured Stefan. Truth had become indistinguishable from untruth and the gulf between reality and illusion grew cavernous. 'The most just woman in the world' had her defence minister executed. 'Our lay god, the man for history and eternity' shot peaceful demonstrators. Stefan worked late into the night to mould the lies and obscure the crimes. The end for him came one Saturday after his staff had left to queue for food. Stefan was alone in the Section, writing a piece on the Bokassa diamond scandal. He reached for a file of clippings at the top of a tall stack. It teetered then collapsed like a house of cards. The columns of untruth fell on him. He was trapped under the weight of lies.

On Monday morning when he was found, his breath was shallow. An ambulance, generally forbidden to sexagenarians, was called and the hospital set his cracked ribs. But the X-ray detected tumours. Stefan had throat cancer and only months to live.

While the nation prepared to spread its wings, his body condemned him to slavery. From the hospital bed he saw himself drinking coffee – real coffee – on the Boulevard St Michel. He wanted to taste fresh croissants and feel the butter run down his chin. He could not let the dream slip unrealized through his fingers; he had to see Paris.

Word about the planned December coup had passed between a select few. Ceauşescu was to be removed. The advice to friends was to lie low: the objective was to change the leader not the system. Christmas was a good time to be out of the country. Stefan's passport was organized. He bought a first-class ticket. At Gara de Nord, where urchins scramble onto arriving trains to search for valuables, he boarded the Orient Express. When the train began to move, with a distant whistle and spastic jerk, he laughed a brittle cry. In the depths of the night, not far from the Hungarian border, he fell asleep dreaming of roof tops and chimney pots. He never awoke.

The revolution which came a few days later was an elaborate *pièce de théâtre*. The Securitate stage-managed the battle. They filled the air with gun fire and faked their own destruction. Their shells ripped into the Fine Arts Museum across the Piata. Their machine-gun fire smashed Flemish and Italian treasures. They set fire to the National Library and half a million books were destroyed. But their Central Committee building, standing on the same square, remained undamaged.

Antonietta didn't want us to sleep in their house. 'Ne marchez pas sur mes plates-bandes,' she said. Don't walk on my flower beds. Instead we stayed in a crumbling art deco hotel downtown where the lobby crawled with cockroaches and prostitutes. An ancient open lift hoisted them silently up the building's core. Snatches of proposition were overheard, in a dozen different tongues, as it drifted from floor to floor. The halls smelt of cheap cigarettes and synthetic scent. After dark the walls wailed.

'We have to help Antonietta,' Zita said, but the next morning she stayed in bed, a pillow over her head, and pleaded, 'Get me an ice pack.' Her night had been disturbed by nightmares. 'I dreamt of being driven all around this bloody country, the car screaming like an old witch, and seeing, what do you call it, road signs for Asia.' She had a headache. Winston too looked forlorn. *His tail* which usually curled in a jaunty corkscrew hung like limp spaghetti. 'You look after her, I can't face it. There's been too much death.' She lit a cigarette. Smoke billowed around the pillow. 'I'll get my hair done instead.'

Antonietta wanted to go to the coast and insisted, in her chattering French, on travelling by train. I queued for tickets with eighty others in an unlit, unventilated booking office. Reservations, which were compulsory, were sold only thirty minutes before the train departed. Behind her barred window the clerk read a newspaper and yawned.

The train was jammed so full that it was impossible to walk in the corridor. At stations, where announcements were preceded by the opening bars of the national anthem 'Wake up, Romania, from your dead sleep', passengers squeezed out through compartment windows. An obese bureaucrat in a crumpled nylon suit and a tie blotched with spilt food slipped a newspaper into his briefcase and picked his teeth. A mother breast-fed her baby and when it wet itself hung the urine-stained pants out the window to dry. On the luggage rack a sack full of raw meat dripped blood on the child's pyjamas. Great heavy parcels wrapped in wax paper or tied in old blankets were heaved into the carriages. They were stacked in the toilets and guarded by peasant women who stared suspiciously through the gap in the door frame. Everywhere boys in pudding-bowl helmets chewed their nails and toyed with Kalashnikovs.

Antonietta wanted Emil, her goldfish, to see the Black Sea. He swam in a bowl on her lap. 'N'ayez pas peur. Don't be frightened. They're men of good faith,' she told him. 'They protect us from terrorists.' Every Romanian had warned us about terrorists and praised men of good faith.

'Who are these people?' I asked.

'Mais t'es fou, hein!' she exclaimed. 'Everyone knows the terrorists are mad dogs. They attack the television station.'

But nobody knew. The press warned of the threat they posed yet left details vague, emotive and malleable. No one questioned the claim. It was as evocative as the unspecified evil in a fairytale.

After the revolution people had demanded the end of the years of 'wooden tongues'. Truth alone must be told. But Stefan and his disciples had reduced the language to rhetoric. The people concluded that new words must be found. But the expressions they coined, cast in the same mould, quickly lost value. Words, the most precious commodity, had been rendered meaningless.

'Terrorists are evil men who wear black and shoot people at night,' explained Antonietta. 'But men of good faith,' she continued, 'it means – I tell you so you do not ask – that you love Romania and will not dishonour the memory of the heroes of the revolution.'

'So I am a man of good faith?'

As she sniggered her hump shook. 'Mais non, tu ne comprends rien. You are a foreigner so maybe you are a terrorist?' She touched my hand, suddenly serious, 'Not really, of course. I know you.'

'Men of good faith', it transpired, were the supporters of the National Salvation Front, the Communists who staged a palace coup and called it a revolution. They had nothing to do with goodness or faith. Equally 'terrorists' had little to do with terror. They simply disagreed with the government. The press, which had remained in the same hands, could print 'Opposition associated with terrorists' and the claim could not be refuted because the word had never been defined. It – like so many others – was twisted to suit immediate political requirements: bourgeoisie, enemy of the people, kulak, terrorist. The deception was accepted without question.

The train stopped with the squeal of unoiled brakes. At Mangalia the rails ran into the Black Sea. The water, aquamarine and cold, lapped against the soft sandy beach. My destination was no longer the end of my trip.

'You're wondering how a hunchback caught such an intellectual,' she said, bowl under arm, as we walked along the shore.

'I know you met on a train.'

'Not on a train. Alors, c'est une histoire vrai et bien amoureuse. I was a stationmaster's daughter. My father, he hated me. "You'll die a virgin," he said. "No one will marry your hump." I told him, "Idiot, I could have a man by the weekend." The jackal laughed like a dog.'

'Et alors, each day the Bucureşti express arrives at our station. Each day I sit on my bench and hitch my skirt a little higher. On

185

Monday I show my ankles, Tuesday, *mes mollets*, on Wednesday afternoon my skirt was above my knees. Good knees, you see? Thursday I showed a little thigh and on Friday . . .' She cackled. '*Et voilà*, on Saturday Stefan stepped off the train and took my hand. He'd seen everything; well, almost everything. He was mine in a week. Who else would have married me, a hunchback,' she asked, 'but a man of good faith?'

Antonietta lifted up the bowl and showed the fish the sea. 'Voilà, mon brave, regardes. Tu es chez-toi.' But the glass inside a goldfish bowl acted as a mirror. The outside world was obscured and the fish only saw what it had always seen, itself.

There was a dark tide in Romanian affairs, a flood of frustration and fear. The country unfolded like Orff's *Carmina Burana*: a rhythm beyond reason, the sound of many individual voices compelled to produce a single voice, discordant, anarchic, demonic and finally, tragically human.

A blue-yellow-and-red Romanian flag, with the hated Communist crest cut out, lazed in the still air above a guard post. For a time it had seemed that the deaths were not in vain, that the thousands killed in December's riots had helped thrust Romania toward reform. At first people spoke openly, political parties debated, independent newspapers were published and democracy thrived. But soon the voices were stifled. The deaths were useless and the sacrifices as insignificant as the scratchings of chickens. Nothing changed. Twilight descended again and the potent symbol of the flag became yet another meaningless token.

MOSCOVY

Communism and Constipation

ANNA KARENINA HAD THROWN herself under a train. I remembered while watching Zita at the window. Had she too been constipated? The carriage toilet had been locked at the border.

'I haven't had a decent movement since we left Berlin,' Zita told the attendant in her flawless Russian. The weeks of pork cutlets and *knödel* had clogged our works. 'What if it comes upon us suddenly?' We were offered tea from the samovar, served in metallic cups which depicted earth and the Kremlin circled by sputniks, but no sympathy. Rules were rules and had to be obeyed.

It was a world full of Kalashnikovs. Soldiers surrounded the train and border guards entered with torches. The lighting had failed.

'Wait in your compartments,' they ordered. We shared ours. A haughty Romanian couple who had treated us with disdain became contrite school children during the customs inspection. The officer scrutinized their declaration.

'Your ring. Is it gold?'

The wife submitted her wedding band for inspection. 'It's nothing special.'

'Where did you buy it?'

'In Romania,' her husband answered. 'It's only Romanian.'

The officer noted the details, stamped the form twice then turned to us. She asked to see our money.

'Have you any gold?'

Zita opened her mouth and pointed at her new Hungarian dentures. The gesture was ignored. 'Have you listed all your valuables? Cameras and watches, currency, stocks and share certificates?' We had. 'Have you a radio receiver or transmitter? Have you anti-Soviet books, magazines or explosives?' We shook our heads. Our forms were stamped twice but she regarded us with suspicion before she passed on to the next compartment.

Two soldiers followed, small caps jammed on the backs of their heads, and motioned us into the corridor. Zita was reluctant to stand but they insisted. The compartment needed to be searched. Their torches played across our companions' possessions, new suitcases wrapped in plastic and tied with rope, and under their seats. Everything seemed in order. They glanced at our luggage. It was still damp. The younger guard tossed his cap aside, dropped to his knees and lifted a bunk to inspect the hold beneath. His light fell on Winston sleeping soundly on a rug and an overdose of Mogadon. The Romanians didn't take well to their huge and unwelcome fellow voyager. The soldiers demanded an explanation but Zita was concerned that Winston not be woken. She kept lowering the bunk only to have it raised again by every official wanting to see the stowaway.

'You've disturbed his sleep,' was all she would say. A veterinary certificate, which we had translated into Russian as a precaution, restored a measure of calm.

'I asked you if you were carrying any food products,' accused the customs officer to which Winston, had he been awake, would have taken offence.

The Romanians insisted on a new compartment and we were thankful for the extra space. The train was airless and filthy. Its windows had been bolted shut. There was a sense of confinement even when the dawn unrolled on an endless, flat landscape. The steppe stretched to the horizon but for all its vastness the biggest country on earth felt small.

By the side of the track the birch trees did not dance. They stood straight and tall in orderly rows at the edge of great plains. 'When the forest is cut down,' the Russians say, 'wood chips fly.' The millions who had perished in the Terror were known as Stalin's chips. Peter had no family left in Russia. His father had been felled. When the police came for him, shortly before dawn, he offered no resistance. 'So he lied to me. He was against the Party all the time,' Peter's mother had said. The police, sombre and bored, asked her to gather her husband's things. She refused. He was, after all, an enemy of the Party. She blocked his way when he went to kiss his sleeping son goodbye. 'My child has no father.' A year later she too died in a labour camp.

The Danubius Express penetrated vast pinewoods then traversed marshlands dotted with bulrushes and water-lilies. White bodies, emerging from hibernation like moles, stood on the prows of wooden boats and plunged into the icy water. Their villages were wooden, the weathered houses of log or plank sprouting home-made television aerials fashioned from wire and tin. Blossoming fruit trees were enclosed by picket fences. On the pastel-yellow platforms of railway stations – all Czarist domes and Byzantine arches – squat women held the hands of thick-thighed boys. Anna Karenina would have recognized them, but the banners – 'Glory to the victorious people' – would not have been familiar.

We had left Bucharest the previous morning. On the road out of town, by the sulphur works, I had driven into a flooded pot-hole and the engine had stalled. It was Zita who noticed the steam rising through the floor. Winston squealed as the car began to sink. We scrambled out and the tarmac split open. I passed out our bags as hot water swirled around my feet. A crowd gathered. The road, already perforated with pot-holes, disintegrated and slowly, like a great liner going down in the north Atlantic, the Trabant sank into the boiling whirlpool. It disappeared from sight. A huge heating culvert had fractured and our vehicle was gone.

It took the rest of the morning to convince my aunt to take the train to Moscow. It was impractical to buy another car, the waiting list was ten years long. On the journey to the border she sat bolt upright and seemed relieved when the Romanians refused us permission to leave. Our papers showed that we had entered the country with a Trabant. We could not leave without it. Our explanation supported by Polaroid photographs did not change their position. If the car really had sunk into the earth, which they did not believe, then we had to return to Bucharest for a form. They were convinced that the car had been sold on the black market and we were offered passage only in exchange for Winston but that, said Zita, was too high a price to pay.

We retired hurt. Zita wanted to be in Moscow by the Victory Day holiday and there wasn't time to return to Bucharest. With a razor blade I cut the offending page from my passport. We caught the next train. The guards had changed. We were waved into the Soviet Union.

On the outskirts of Moscow Zita emerged from the fetid toilet wafting Roger et Gallet soap and puffs of scented powder. Her sparse hair was gathered in a bow. She announced her intention to see Lenin.

'He's dead, Zita.'

'You could have fooled me.' Outside the window, in the shadow of the ubiquitous tower blocks, banners still flew his portrait. Picnickers sat by great steam heating pipes, his image pinned over their hearts, his profile guarding their newspapers' mast-heads. But soon he would be dead and gone for ever.

'Your uncle and I tried to visit his mausoleum but without much success. This time nothing will get in my way.'

The Danubius rolled into Kievski station. The journey from Romania had taken thirty hours but we had arrived in time. It was 9 May, Victory Day, the celebration of the end of the Great Patriotic War and the anniversary of Peter and Zita's union.

'On time.' Sasha met us crackling like a charged capacitor. When he spoke, the discharge shook his whole body and sparks flew from his fingertips. 'Always on time. No bread in the shops but the trains run on time.'

I asked why.

'You never ask why in the Soviet Union. Why is not a question.' He gestured at Winston. 'Very wise – you'll make a good profit on the black market.' Winston regarded our host with suspicion. Zita tried to explain about the harem. 'But I have good contacts,' he persisted. 'We could be paid in dollars.' When she refused Sasha laughed until his head seemed fit to burst. He didn't seem to believe us.

To hail a cab in Moscow one steps into the street and sticks out a hand, not for a taxi, they rarely stop, but for a private car.

A battered Moscovitch pulled up immediately. Sasha opened the door and requested an address. The driver only revved the engine.

'Five roubles,' offered Sasha.

'Ten.'

'Seven.'

The tariff agreed, the driver suggested driving by way of the Rizhki street market where everything from wedding dresses to Ukranian peaches can be bought for a price. It was the ideal place to sell a pig. But he accepted our refusal without question and agreed to carry Winston on the back seat as if it were the most common request.

The car pulled away before Sasha had closed the door and before the Miliman, beating his leg idly with a white truncheon, reached us.

'Sometimes trucks, even ambulances offer a lift. It's illegal, of course,' said Sasha, 'but taxis don't stop. It's understandable; they make more money selling vodka.'

Only fools made assumptions in Moscow. All private cars were for hire and taxis sold vodka. Soviet citizens were guaranteed jobs but no one survived on a single salary. Everyone was forced to moonlight. Our driver, an engineer judging by the technical manuals under our feet, had clocked into work, hung his coat on his chair and left the office to drive a cab all morning to supplement his income. 'We pretend to work and they pretend to pay us,' went the saying.

'Stalin pulled down the trees.' The Moscovitch rattled us around the dusty Garden Ring Road. 'Moscow used to be the city of forty forties, there were sixteen hundred churches here before the revolution. Now there are one hundred. The helmsman of our destiny pulled those down too.' Gothic limestone sand castles glowered where golden onion domes once had gleamed. Stalin's seven Gormenghast skyscrapers were visions from a nightmare. 'Byvayet,' shrugged Sasha. It happens. His humour had an anarchic irony.

Zita asked after an elegant building.

'That used to be the residence of Kremlin officials,' Sasha told us.

'Who lives there now?'

'Their families; it's been turned over to the people. And here's the Swimming Pool of Christ the Saviour.' The impromptu tour continued. 'Stalin demolished Moscow's great cathedral, the church of Christ the Saviour and proposed that a magnificent palace of Socialism be built in its place. The foundations were laid but, lo and behold, they sank. So they laid them again and they sank again. How the church had stood on the land for a hundred years no one could answer but their palace could not replace it. The land would support nothing heavier than a swimming pool.' Sasha leaned over the seat and whispered, 'But they say it's impossible to drown there.'

Outside a shop next door a queue swayed slightly before a rosy notice: 'All for you.'

The propaganda called it a hero city infinitely dear to all the Soviet people but Moscow's sweeping scale – broad boulevards, faceless blocks, the sinister symmetrical university – diminished the individual. It was familiar yet foreign, an Asian city in Europe and a European capital in Asia. The Kremlin, the hub of city and empire, was described by concentric circles: by the Sadovoye Koltso orbital road which was originally a sixteenth-century defensive line, by the Golden Ring of the towns Zagorsk, Vladimir and Suzdal, by her republics, by the curve of Latvia, Lithuania and Ruthenia, by the orbit of satellites Poland, Czechoslovakia, Hungary and Romania. In five hundred years the little principality of Moscovy had grown into an immense empire which came to control one sixth of the globe. We had penetrated its defences and drove into its rotten core.

'But today it's different.' We turned into a grim street of foundries and smoke. Chaussée of the Enthusiasts was once called the Vladimirsky Highway: from here the Czar's exiles began their walk to Siberia. It had started to rain. 'We have *perestroika*. See the difference.' Sasha pointed out the grimy window. The line of factory gates were decked in bedraggled flags. 'Before *perestroika* all the banners were red. Now we have pluralism: yellow flags, green flags, blue flags.' The driver stopped to put on the wipers. They had been in the glove compartment. Left on the windscreen they would have been stolen. Behind him a powder-blue poster read 'Have a nice holiday, comrades'.

'You're here for Victory Day, of course. The parade. Thanks to the Party we are victorious.' Sasha blew a raspberry. 'It's easy to satirize the Soviet Union for its reality is so absurd. But at least, now, we can make money.' Our destination lay beneath another banner. 'A hearty welcome to war vets.' The car came to a stop.

'Plus an extra rouble for the pig,' demanded the driver.

Change, Sasha believed, was life's only constant. He knew that fortune favoured the brave. Opportunities had to be exploited. Everyone was doing it. It was the new philosophy, almost a new dogma. His father felt differently. He craved the absolute. He was a Russian. His son had read too much Western trash.

When Byzantium fell, Moscovy became the world's only Orthodox state. Encircled by its enemies, Mongol Khans, Turkish Beys, Swedish feudal lords and Polish Sarmatians, the kingdom was shaped under a messianic idea: the faith had to be defended at all costs. While Western Christianity evolved with Greek philosophy, the Moscovites granted reform no quarter. Scepticism remained an anathema and the divine word was not tempered by man's doubt. To protect they attacked. Moscovy's army marched for the west in 1500 and, in a sense, never stopped marching. The absolutes of communism seized the Russian spirit like the certainties of Orthodoxy. The new dogma melded with the old. The Kremlin had a new crusade. It acted both from its duty as the first socialist state and its pride as heir of the true faith. Workers, like the priests before them, led the masses of the world toward emancipation and no one in the Party, Sasha's father included, had yet accepted the need to adapt. The giant leviathan rattled its final death throes.

Styopa held up a glass. 'Drinking is the joy of the Rus. We cannot live without it.' His lyrical voice had a suggestion of tears and a wave of melancholy seemed to flood over the room when he spoke. 'I toast the memory of Vladimir of Kiev who rejected Islam.' The glass vanished in his fleshy paw and its contents down his throat. 'Good vodka.' He smacked his lips. His teeth were red gold, the same colour as his wedding ring. 'Someone paid dearly.'

'And in dollars. But I prefer whisky.'

'My son is no Russian,' Styopa complained to Zita then turned back to Sasha. 'No one likes the taste of vodka. You drink only to get drunk.' He demonstrated with a second glass: exhale, swallow in one, then smell the inside of your elbow to kill the acerbity. 'Farewell, then, dear comrade Peter, you fought to the last, your name lives eternally in our hearts . . .' It went on. Russian toasts tended to be long-winded.

My aunt and uncle had met Styopa years before at his retirement party. His employers at the Laboratory of Biological Structure (or VNIIGrob, the All-Union Scientific Research Institute for Graves, as those in the know liked to tease) wished to honour his contribution to the science. Stalin was long dead and a proletarian lineage was no longer a prerequisite for survival. Over Armenian cognac Styopa confessed to his suspicion of noble pedigree. He told Zita that an ancestor had been a châtelaine in the court of Catherine the Great. At the time of the wars against the Turks she was betrothed to an Austrian colonel. But the princely soldier was expelled from Russia by the Czarina and deserted the fair châtelaine. Yet their brief liaison was not without issue. Styopa's forefather was born with the curious but endearing deformity of misaligned ears. Zita reassured Styopa on his suspicions of nobility then said nothing more, but she cherished the secret bond of blood which coursed through their veins.

The flat was cluttered with a lifetime's scavenging. Styopa was a collector, a picaroon, incapable of passing a tip without a good rootle. All his life he had hoarded. He abhorred waste. The Soviet Union's two major newspapers were *Pravda*, the Truth, and *Izvestia*, the News. Both were published by the Party. It was said that in the News there is no truth and in the Truth there is no news. Styopa had kept every issue from the last seventeen years. They were heaped from floor to ceiling with magazines, stuffed birds, old clock mechanisms and a petrol pump. Boxes of postcards crammed broken escritoires. A Pathé movie camera and rusting tins of Sovkino out-takes, which might have been cut by Sergi Eisenstein, reduced the broad living room to a narrow passageway. The other rooms could be reached only through a labyrinth of tunnels. Yet the chaotic warren was not disorganized and Styopa could recall the location of every item. His memory was remarkable. He knew by heart every photograph in every magazine, every article in all his newspapers. Their dates were the hooks on which his life was hung.

A dusty television had been unearthed from behind a stack of books. A tube had blown and could not be replaced but the set still worked although its picture was distorted. Soldiers with elongated torsos marched on stubby legs across the screen. Towering rockets were carried on Lilliputian launchers. The Politburo, with lofty foreheads and no chins, raised in salute great long arms from shrunken bodies. The Red Army, part dwarf, part giant, canted past the review stand. '*Urra!*' roared the contracted troops at a stretched portrait of Lenin.

In Gorki Park veterans met, reminisced and wept vodka tears. Some carried hand-written signs asking, 'Were you with the 24th Tank Corps in Tatsinskaya?' and 'Sailor from the Kirov: any shipmates?' They ate ice cream and, under the banner 'Glory to the Victorious People', accepted red tulips from Pioneers. Then they returned home with their medals and memories. So ended the last great Victory Day parade, in emptiness and defeat.

The broadcast was followed by an advertisement for a Western product. Never before had Soviet television shown a commercial. It was qualified by a caption: 'All these goods can be obtained for freely convertible currency.' Dollars. If you don't have dollars in Moscow you go hungry. If you don't queue you starve. Only a few months before, the Soviet Union's first billboard had appeared. 'Coke . . . it's the real thing' flashed in neon above Pushkin Square. Cola sales soared. The *apparatchiki* embraced the spirit, if not the substance, of advertising. They concluded that marketing held no mysteries and launched a series of their own campaigns. 'Tula Combine Harvesters . . . it's the real thing' and 'Melodiya Records . . . it's the real thing'. Their advertisements produced disappointing results.

Styopa buried the television again behind the encyclopaedias. Beyond the undercarriage of a Yakovlev was a still. The vodka had been drunk and Styopa, like most Russians, distilled *samogon* from potatoes, beets, cabbage, any food in fact which contained sugar. The liquor was called 'Komsomol girl's tears' and tasted like fermented dust.

'He died of syphilis. Did I ever tell you?'

'I'm not bloody surprised,' choked Zita. 'No one should drink this poison. I'm going teetotal.'

'No, I mean Vladimir Ilych.' Lenin. 'It is not a state secret any more.'

'It isn't surprising considering he screwed a whole country,' added Sasha.

'My son,' Styopa pointed a stubby finger, 'would not speak like this were Stalin alive. He was a good man. A man who feared God.'

'Is that why he destroyed the churches?'

'That wasn't Stalin, that was the vulture Beria. When Stalin was alive life was hard but good. There was food in the shops. There was order then.'

'Did you do him too?' Zita asked.

'Yes, I had the honour, but no sooner had we finished than Khrushchev took him out of the mausoleum and had him buried. My greater work was on Lenin.'

First came the strokes. Lenin lost control of his foot. His right side became paralysed. He developed problems speaking and expressing his thoughts. He was confined to bed and speech therapy prescribed. One cold night in January the convulsions began. His pulse increased to 130, his breathing to thirty-six gasps a minute. The doctors tried morphine and his temperature soared from 42.3° centigrade to beyond the end of the thermometer. The fits decreased for a moment. Then, just before seven in the morning, blood rushed to his head, his face turned violet, he took a deep breath and died. Artificial resuscitation, attempted for twenty-five minutes, was unsuccessful.

'They embalmed him the next day,' Styopa told us, 'with disinfecting liquid – a mixture of formalin and medical spirit – via the aeorta. His brain was removed and preserved in the Lenin Museum. It weighed, as I recall, 1340 grams, a little smaller than normal but that was the effect of the disease.'

Lenin's widow, Nadezhda Konstantinovna, was appalled that her husband was to be displayed like a stuffed trophy. She wrote to *Pravda* saying that the monument he wanted was money for hospitals and schools.

'But Vladimir Ilych had to be preserved from oblivion.'

After the war Styopa was engaged as a senior technician. 'When I began, the body was in a poor state.' His expertise was the use of electricity. 'In the early days they had few technical resources. Now our laboratory on Krasin Street is the most advanced in the world.'

He worked closely with plastic surgeons and skin-graft specialists. 'The best, only the best.' A new partial-vacuum glass sarcophagus helped inhibit decay but Styopa's shock treatment reversed it.

'Once every two or three months a high voltage charge was applied to keep up the tone. But the first time we tried it I overestimated the power needed. Lenin suddenly sat up from the table, his arms shook and his lips started to quiver. I thought he was going to speak. It was quite a shock. After that we reduced the voltage.'

'But it's been seventy years. What really can be left of him?'

'Ah,' he said, only 'ah' and poured more drink.

Sasha suggested that it was time to bury the leading spirit of the revolution.

'All you radicals', warned Styopa, 'will end up like Dmitri the False Czar.' In the seventeenth century Dmitri encouraged reform and was murdered by the people. They fired his remains from a cannon in Red Square.

'My father has no interest in politics,' his son explained. 'He has his pictures to occupy him.'

'It's just a hobby.'

The hobby was an obsession. We hadn't noticed the collages for the clutter. The walls, where they could be seen, were hung with his remarkable work. Styopa collected precious mementos, arranged them layer by layer into three-dimensional compositions and sealed them in polyester-resin moulds. Each layer, of which there were at least eight, was meticulously composed. Delicate lace overlay alternatively obscured and revealed a

myriad of relics – ikons and clock springs, Botticelli virgins and
Soviet workers, autumn leaves and silver bullets. Stars glittered
above shards of ultramarine porcelain. Mirrors with tinted gels
created the impression of depth and transformed the glass boxes
into luminous prisms. When sunlight fell on his collages rain-
bows danced on the wall.

He had made them chronologically. The subject of each was
a year. Major events were represented by a token and the tokens
evoked memories. I held in my hand golden 1945. A gilded
Stalin, flanked by grateful peasants, trampled evil underfoot. Red
flags from a set of tin soldiers marched while Prokofiev's Cinder-
ella danced and a new world dawned.

'It was a bloody joy to be a Communist then,' recalled Zita,
'to serve humanity, being present at the birth of a better future.'

Black death and silver tears coloured 1953: Stalin had died,
Beria was shot. The year 1956 was red and blue, Union Jack and
sabres: the British in Suez, the CND at Aldermaston, terrorists
in Cyprus. There was no mention of the Soviet invasion of Hungary, but then memory, like art, has no morality.

The theme that ran throughout was time. 'Difficulties arise
when history is reassessed,' admitted Styopa. 'I did Khrushchev
in 1962 when he was a hero but now he is disgraced. What do I
do? I cannot remove him without destroying the whole picture.'
As each layer hardened, heated from the chemical reaction, any
fault might fracture the whole piece and destroy the relics. The
process could be heartbreaking. A month's work might splinter
before his eyes.

I suggested that his work would be appreciated in the West.
Styopa only shrugged. 'I have been to America. I did not like
it.' Then he picked up a sod of imaginary earth and pronounced,
'The Russian soil,' as an Irishman would eulogize 'the Irish turf'.
Styopa would say no more. Sasha was admiring Winston, men-
tally dividing him into different cuts of meat. Outside, shrieking
stars of fireworks burst above Red Square and Gorki Park. Voices
from other windows cheered, 'Urra! Glory to the Communist
Party! We are victorious!' I couldn't tell if they were being
sarcastic.

The *samogon* too was finished. There had been no sugar in the shops and his cellar, a line of flagons and firkins under a stringless grand piano, ran dry. Styopa proposed a competition. We would recite poetry and whoever faltered first had to buy the vodka. He began with Lermontov, a cry from the depths of the Caucasus. Sasha cheated by mouthing a rhyming Stalinist slogan, 'Winter has past, Summer has come, thanks to the Party for that.' When we objected he countered with lines of Pushkin. Zita surprisingly chose Tannhäuser, the minstrel whose starry-eyed idealists were forced to face earthly reality.

> For many a thing done in my youth
> I sore do now repine;
> If I had known better what I know now,
> Far better light were mine.
> My inward self I then knew not,
> Thus must I pay dearly.

Then it was my turn. I hesitated and lost. Zita and Sasha offered to accompany me.

'Don't forget the *avoska*.' A string carrier bag. Every Russian carried one everywhere. The word had been derived from *avos* or 'just in case'. It was a means of coping with the erratic supply of goods.

Styopa said he would nap until our return and lay down with Winston under the piano among back issues of *Sobriety and Culture*. As we left, the deep gloom, no longer suspended by the veil of drink, again descended on the flat.

It was after midnight. A taxi stopped hoping that we might buy his wares. We also wanted a ride and the driver made an exception. It wasn't possible to drive ourselves as the wheels of Styopa's Lada had been stolen the previous night. The car lay in the gutter like a whale washed up on a beach.

As the taxi drove down Gorki Street toward Red Square the street lights dimmed. The holiday was over and a great mural of Lenin was dismantled. Flags were plucked from lamp posts like spines from a porcupine and hurled into trucks. The wartime atmosphere returned. Moscow was again a city under siege. It was as if a squadron of enemy bombers was expected overhead at any moment.

'My father doesn't like to talk about his trip to America,' explained Sasha. 'A gallery in New York had seen his work and they offered to exhibit it. It was like a dream come true. So my father bought a ticket – it cost him all his savings – and chose the five pictures, the maximum he could take out of the country. You see in the People's State everything belongs to the people. Even your paintings or sculptures are not your own, they are the people's. He had the pictures photographed and filled out many, many permits and took them to the Culture Ministry to be stamped. He gave the *apparatchik* a box of chocolates to ease the task. It was normal.

'So the big day came. I took him to Sheremetyevo, the airport. We kissed. He was happy. But when they checked his export papers they found one hadn't been stamped. One out of fifty. It was an oversight, obviously, but it didn't matter. His pictures couldn't leave the country. He could go but his pictures would stay.' Sasha sighed. 'He went, of course, what else could he do? He couldn't change his flight. He couldn't wait another year for a new visa. And in New York the gallery wasn't interested: what good is an artist without paintings? My father stayed one week at the YMCA then flew home, back into the arms of mother Russia.'

We paid the driver, not the meter reading but an agreed price, and walked up the perfect cobbles into Red Square. 'Glory to the Victorious People' had been rolled up, the review stand dismantled and the litter from the parade hosed away. A lean officer adorned in a foundry of medals eased a barrel-shaped wife from the path of the street sweepers.

The Kremlin towered before us. Heroic red flags cracked against an ink-black sky. A sign warned that smoking was forbidden. The bells of St Basil's, a floodlit swirl of onion domes like twists of blown glass, rang tunelessly. The building was no longer a church. It had been deconsecrated. There could be only one temple on Red Square.

Lenin's mausoleum squatted like a red marble toad. 'I need to see him. I never managed while Peter was alive.' Zita wore 'Victory' on a lapel badge.

'He has the day off today, everyone does, but we can come tomorrow. You remember Stalin is no longer in there.'

Stalin had himself interned in the mausoleum like an Egyptian pharaoh. His name appeared above Lenin's – and in bigger letters – until Khrushchev took it down and stuck the body in the Kremlin wall with the others.

'They loved him and still do. Fresh flowers are placed on his grave every day: every day and only on *his* grave. Yet he sent more to their deaths than Hitler and all his concentration camps.'

Blossoms blew down Marx Prospect and were caught, like butterflies in a net, by a banner advising 'Protect children from unpleasant circumstances'.

'Maybe it seems to you in the West', Sasha continued, 'that it's time to forget about the Second World War, about the labour camps. But for us it is essential to uncover the past. The truth is more important than bread.' Before the war Russia had not been a great power. The revolution and the Terror had sapped its strength. Stalin, through cunning and tyranny, transformed the Union into a superpower. He built the world's greatest empire on Russian autocratic tradition.

'He once said, "Gaiety is the most outstanding feature of the Soviet Union." ' We were standing outside the Children's World store, its windows full of cuddly bears and *matryoshki* dolls. 'Maybe that's why he built the toy shop here.' Across Dzerzhinski Square stood the Lubyanka, the dirty yellow glazed Czarist prison and home of the KGB. 'To remind the people that they are children.'

Power depends on a willingness of the public to submit. At first Lenin hadn't seen the need for a secret police force. The dreaded Okhrana was disbanded. But he soon realized that 'a special system of organized violence' was necessary to establish the dictatorship of the proletariat. One of their first victims was a celebrated circus clown Bim-Bom whose repertoire included jokes about the Communists. Agents advanced on him during a show and the audience, delighted by the innovation, applauded the performance. But their pleasure was cut short as the gunmen opened fire and Bim-Bom fled from the ring.

Children needed protection. Militants sent ten million kulaks to their deaths. Private farming was forbidden. In the subsequent famine a further seven million peasants perished. During the war KGB troops deported or murdered whole minorities: the Balkars, Chechens, Ingushi, Kalmyks, Karachai, Crimean Tartars and Volga Germans. They were different. They were dangerous. Our children needed protection. The Party always knew best.

Zitochka he called her. Little Zita. It was their forty-fifth anniversary too.

Multiple sclerosis was diagnosed shortly after Peter's second fall. He had brought Zita to Red Square to see Lenin but collapsed on the mausoleum's polished marble steps. The doctors told him to take a rest and leave was approved. All too soon he needed a stick, then crutches. The paralysis crept up his legs like dry rot, gnawing away at his nerve fibres. He was plagued by double vision and lost control of his bladder. Once a GTO ('Ready for Labour and Defence') gold badge athlete, he could no longer stand unaided. At night he whispered, 'Zitochka, are you there?' and all the time her hand had been resting on his thigh.

Peter's fear was not physical incapacity, it was shame. No one resigns from the KGB, but his heart had gone out of the work. He was allowed to decrease his responsibilities until there was nothing to keep him in Moscow and they boarded an aircraft for Berlin. Never again would they travel together by train, never again would they make love in the tunnels, not on the Praga or Leningrad Express, the Pushkin or Maestral. They slid into furious frustrated retirement in the rambling house in Potsdam. It was a curious destination for a Russian. 'He chose Germany because he needed to fight,' Zita told me. 'Your uncle was mad with life.' Anger kept him alive until a falling pig snapped his neck.

She shook her head. 'I'm the last of the line. There was only me and Peter. Now there's no one. The family's dead and buried and good riddance to them.'

Victory, victory to the glorious people. On the night of an earlier anniversary I had found Zita standing alone by the garden gate with tears of pain rolling down her face. Her infected teeth had yet to be removed and their toxin had poisoned her body. Her legs and arms were pocked with ulcers. That morning Peter had fallen and broken both legs. How old can we get, she was asking. 'Life,' she sighed, 'some pay a double bill for it.'

On Dzerzhinski Square I demanded of Sasha, 'Who is responsible?'

'Not me,' he answered.

'Every Soviet citizen says he's not responsible, the truth is you are all responsible.' A union bonded by fear.

'It isn't that Russians are afraid to speak, we're afraid to think. Tell us to salivate like Pavlov's dogs or lie under tanks and we will. We will. *Urra!* Eastern Europe will recover. They've had communism for only forty years. Dostoevsky said to destroy a nation took two generations – seventy years. That's today,' he said urgently. 'It's seventy years since the glorious October Revolution. We are the beheaded country. This is the cemetery of intellectuals.' Take all the horrors of the old eastern bloc, multiply it by one hundred and you have the tragedy of the Soviet people. 'We are waking from sleep into a crazy world, all smoke and mirrors. It's such an effort to begin to understand but it's so important. We have so little time.'

Hell may resemble the Moscow Metro: flawless and sterile. The escalator bore us deep down into Satan's Versailles, a subterranean palace of blast doors and trains which run on time. Beautifully crafted lies embellished the walls. Beneath the mosaics of loyal workers, offering their labours – rifles, tractors and loaves – to an altar of red flags, the masses had moved silently during Stalin's Terror. In grand marble tunnels the only sound was their shuffling feet. Loiterers were brushed aside. Nothing would delay the heroic march. The world wept grey tears when communism was victorious.

We waited no more than half a minute. A silver train whisked us through the burial grounds of a civilization as dead as Rome.

*

Our room was beyond Styopa's collection of typewriters. Galleys of machines, many without keys or rollers, had been stacked to form a vault, a sort of annalistic arch. Beyond them I sat on the toilet, with little success, and stared at a faded photograph pinned to the back of the door. A young man in uniform and a woman in cotton dress waltzed on a bombed-out street. They laughed in the ruins. Underneath the caption '9 May 1945' had been typed. I didn't understand. After the *gulags*, after Auschwitz, after the betrayal and deception, the humiliation and lies, how does a man live again? Haunted by nightmares, plagued by memory, how does one cope with the horror? Only, it seemed, through our capacity to forget.

I found Zita in bed, mirror in hand, hair unbrushed. 'Who do you see?' she asked. I told her. She shook her head. 'There are two people: the me you know and the someone else that nobody knows, the someone who I'd completely forgotten.' She put down the glass. Winston stirred at her feet. 'Something unbelievable happened at the end of the war. Suddenly there was this beautiful future stretching out before us and that terrible past could be left behind. Life seemed to be a piece of cheesecake. But because we didn't ruddy well feel responsible for what had happened, the present became a desert and everything. It wasn't someone else's fault – it was our own,' she said. 'Those poor people, those poor bloody people.' I turned out the light. We heard the wail of a love-sick cat and the distant rumble of parade convoys returning to barracks; tank tracks on asphalt. Zita addressed the darkness. 'You forgot to wish me happy anniversary.'

That night she dreamt of Berlin. She came out of her house, out from behind the gate, and walked into town. She was naked but it didn't matter as the streets were deserted. She saw the city as it had been, no longer divided, whole once again. The Wall, Peter's wall, had been dismantled. Express trains from Paris to Moscow and from St Petersburg to Prague ran through the great stations without let or hindrance. Slowly Zita became aware that she wasn't alone. There were other people, thousands and thousands of people, on the streets. She panicked, covered herself and scurried back behind the garden gate. But she realized that they too were naked and they roared, a great belly laugh of relief, and greeted her in her true name, naked together at the heart of Europe.

Where was the end of Europe? The Czechs felt Asia began over the Morava. Hungarians pointed at Romania. Poles looked no further than suburban Praga. The Russians, for their part, believed that the Urals, Siberia and even Vladivostok on the Pacific were all European. But wherever the border lay it no longer followed the Iron Curtain. That heinous and false division of east and west became an historical aberration. Europe was whole again. We were one family, I realized, responsible not only for the grace of golden Prague and the blue of Voroneţ but for the ashen evil of Auschwitz and the blooded linen sheets of Budapest. It was a collective burden. Why should a pampered Western boy be exempt from liability?

A Pig in the Hand

IT RAINED THE NEXT MORNING. I agreed to meet Zita by the Lenin mausoleum at midday and set out for OVIR – the Department of Visas and Registration. My visa needed to be inspected. On my arrival there was already a long queue and I waited with the others in the wet. The intercom crackled intermittently. Only one person at a time was allowed to pass through the electric gate and into the building. The system was inefficient. The name of each country was anounced and its nationals, if any, went forward. It was the illogical logic of Moscow.

As the second hour passed I grew nervous, I didn't want to be late for Lenin. When the intercom next crackled I jumped the queue. Inside the bureau ice-blue eyes and cropped blond hair awaited me. A security monitor flickered behind him. He inspected my passport, which wasn't Norwegian, and ordered me outside. I explained in English.

'Outside, pleeze, Outside,' he insisted. I stepped back into the hall. 'Outside, pleeze.' I retreated onto the porch. At least I would be dry. 'Outside, outside.' The ice-blue eyes drove me back down the steps, across the courtyard, through the gate and onto the street.

I needed to register that morning. The instructions demanded it. When the intercom next crackled a Japanese tourist didn't understand so I translated. It was the same with the next announcement. I appointed myself keeper of the gate. 'France,' I parroted. Then, 'Portugal.' Would they never call me? I resembled the Czech greengrocer who hung in his shop window, among the onions and carrots, the slogan 'Workers of the World, unite!'. Like him I was not particularly enthusiastic about unity among workers but wanted to signal to the authorities – the man

with the ice-blue eyes – my willingness to conform. I was
afraid and fear made me obey. I became the *kapo* at Auschwitz,
the driver of transports into Kolyma. I buried the bodies of
the Polish officers executed at Katyń. I was the clerk who
wanted an easy life and a weekend cottage on Lake Balaton.
I despised myself, but jumped forward when my country was
called. My visa was stamped. I thanked ice-blue eyes. He
looked at me in contempt.

The line for the mausoleum, which crooked at wild angles on
the whim of its wardens, cast geometric shadows across the
cobbles. The rain had let up and Sasha was sharing a joke with
Zita.

'Our society's achievements have been made possible by following the dictates of the Party.'

Sasha shrugged in mock helplessness. 'But Comrade, I was
only following orders.'

Pigs, even those on a lead, were not allowed on Red Square
so we left ours in Sasha's care. Winston's initial unease with our
host had passed. He had grown comfortable under Sasha's lavish
attention.

'What the blazes do you think he dreams of?' asked Zita as she
looked back at Winston. As usual she answered her question
herself. 'Not the back seat of a Trabant, that's for certain. He
probably dreams of growing fat on acorns and roots in green
meadows. Or that harem of sows. Lucky beggar.'

I told Zita that after leaving OVIR I had crossed a small
park. Like every other park in the old communist bloc it had
a heroic statue. This one was of Lenin. But the face had been
crushed in by a sledge hammer and the reinforcing rods splayed
like a mad spider's web. A squad of soldiers, Ministry of
Interior troops whose duties included public order, idled
beneath the fractured head. They were armed with submachine
guns. One spoke English. I asked him if they were worried
about social unrest.

'No,' said the captain. 'We are on training exercise. These are
not real guns, not real bullets.'

'Kashmar,' whispered my aunt. Nightmare.

We joined the angular queue. Young Pioneers mimed their allegiance and left bunches of red flowers on the marble steps. We followed the bob of their white bows past motionless sentries, chosen for their similar appearance, and descended into the dim crypt. Twelve guards surrounded the effigy, their bodies rigid but their eyes never still. Lenin reclined in his glass coffin. His left hand lay out flat and his right fist was folded over his black suit. The waxen face and hands were illuminated by discreet spotlights. Beneath the black and red marble, friezed with red flag inlay, Zita hesitated and the queue bunched up behind her. A Pioneer in blue skirt and white knee socks stepped on her heel and dropped a red sash. Zita seemed about to speak then decided against it. An arm firmly took hold and moved her on.

'I looked up to him, you know. I put him on a pedal stool.' In the sun her walk seemed freer. 'He had all the answers, like your uncles. I liked that because it meant I didn't have to think – and thinking is so bloody hard.' It was as if my aunt had slipped back into her body after years of absence. 'It's not just love that's blind – it's bloody me. I loved them both; but they frightened me.' She eased into her own footsteps. 'I'm tired, tired and older than I care to remember. You may take us home now.'

But Sasha wasn't where we had left him. He and Winston had vanished into the crowd. They were nowhere to be seen.

'Oh my God.' Zita stopped in her tracks. 'This is unbelievable.' She was suddenly concerned. 'Just don't say anything, don't say a bloody thing.'

I said nothing as I had to leave my aunt for a moment. My bowels were finally on the move. I hastened to GUM, the galleried Czarist department store, its shelves empty but for cellophane raincoats and alloy busts of Dzerzhinski, and down the steps into the subterranean lavatory. Thankfully, a cabinet was free. I paid my ten kopeks, collected the token length of toilet paper and settled down. When I regained my composure a few moments later, I heard the cries. In the next cubicle a little boy wept. 'Papa . . . Papa . . .' The door was locked. He couldn't open the latch. His father had vanished. A doctor and I tried to force the door but it was jammed shut. Others stood around and watched. They warned us not to break it down. The correct official had to be found but the correct official could not be found. It was lunch hour. They started to argue. I left them to it. I climbed the stairs, the trapped child's cries ringing through the tiled hall, and walked into the fresh air.